PHILADELPHIA

In the *Pennsylvania History Series,*

edited by BEVERLY C. TOMEK and ALLEN DIETERICH-WARD

RECENT TITLES IN THIS SERIES:

Judith Ann Giesberg, *Keystone State in Crisis:
The Civil War in Pennsylvania*

G. Terry Madonna, *Pivotal Pennsylvania: Presidential Politics
from FDR to the Twenty-First Century*

Karen Guenther, *Sports in Pennsylvania*

Marion Winifred Roydhouse, *Women of Industry and Reform:
Shaping the History of Pennsylvania, 1865–1940*

Daniel K. Richter, *Native Americans' Pennsylvania*

This map of Philadelphia shows the city's sections and selected neighborhoods. (Created by Karen L. Wysocki for Frederic M. Miller, Morris J. Vogel, and Allen F. Davis, *Philadelphia Stories: A Photographic History, 1920–1960* [Philadelphia: Temple University Press, 1988]. Copyright © 1988 by Temple University Press. Reprinted by permission of Temple University Press.)

ROGER D. SIMON

PHILADELPHIA

A BRIEF HISTORY

Revised and Updated Edition

TEMPLE UNIVERSITY PRESS
Philadelphia • Rome • Tokyo

TEMPLE UNIVERSITY PRESS
Philadelphia, Pennsylvania 19122
www.temple.edu/tempress

Published by Temple University Press in partnership with The Pennsylvania Historical
  Association

Library of Congress Cataloging-in-Publication Data

Names: Simon, Roger D., author.
Title: Philadelphia : a brief history / Roger D. Simon.
Description: Revised and updated edition. | Philadelphia : Temple University
  Press, 2017. | Series: Pennsylvania history series | Includes bibliographical references
  and index.
Identifiers: LCCN 2016051469 (print) | LCCN 2016054557 (ebook) | ISBN
  9781932304268 (paperback : alkaline paper) | ISBN 9781932304275 (E-Book)
Subjects: LCSH: Philadelphia (Pa.)—History.
Classification: LCC F158.3 .S56 2017 (print) | LCC F158.3 (ebook) | DDC
  974.8/11—dc23
LC record available at https://lccn.loc.gov/2016051469

Design by Kate Nichols

♾ The paper used in this publication meets the requirements of the American National
Standard for Information Sciences—Permanence of Paper for Printed Library Materi-
als, ANSI Z39.48-1992

Printed in the United States of America

9 8 7 6 5 4 3

For

Layna, Jordan, Matthew

CONTENTS

EDITORS' FOREWORD

O N BEHALF OF THE MEMBERS AND OFFICERS of the Pennsylvania Historical Association, we are delighted to present the first volume in the newly redesigned *Pennsylvania History Series* (*PHS*). The *PHS* mission is to provide timely, relevant, high-quality scholarship in a compact and accessible form. Produced by and for scholars engaged in the teaching of Pennsylvania history, books in the series are targeted toward students and intended for use in both the classroom and broader public history settings. Our new partnership with Temple University Press brings the expertise and resources of a respected academic publisher to a book series that has been in existence since the late 1940s and includes more than thirty titles.

This new publication of Roger D. Simon's *Philadelphia: A Brief History* presents a fully revised and updated edition of one of the most popular *PHS* titles. Beginning with the region's first inhabitants, the volume traces the history of a city that became synonymous with the birth of a nation before developing into one of the commercial and intellectual hubs of the Atlantic World. As Simon narrates the city's rise, fall, and postindustrial rebirth, he pays particular attention to how race, class, gender, and other factors shaped the lived experiences of its inhabitants. The book's central premise, that Philadelphia's story is about residents' attempts to sustain economic prosperity while fulfilling community needs, remains as relevant today as it was when William Penn sought to create a utopian "greene Country towne" while still turning a profit on his new colony.

In addition to offering our gratitude to the members of the *PHS* Editorial Board listed below, we thank Roger Simon for being such a great sport as we stumbled through the transition from pie-in-the-sky academics to hard-nosed editors. Roger graciously acceded to most of our requests, including painful cuts to his first draft, while cheerfully refusing to compromise on anything he felt might weaken the volume. We also gratefully acknowledge the work of our editorial predecessors, particularly Diane Wenger, whose efforts during a difficult time kept the series alive and set the stage for its present revival. Thanks also go to Brenda Kern of Waveline Direct, LLC, for designing the series logo and to Vicky Simmel of Gannon Associates Insurance for her many efforts on our behalf. Finally, we owe a debt of gratitude to our new partners at Temple University Press for agreeing to take on this series even though it meant providing a crash course to a couple of wannabe book publishers. Mary Rose Muccie has been a strong supporter of the project since we first approached her with the idea, and she maintained that enthusiasm as we hammered out myriad contractual details. Aaron Javsicas has been a patient and perceptive mentor, and we are delighted to be able to take advantage of the talents of the rest of the Temple University Press staff, including Kate Nichols, who designed the book's cover.

—ALLEN DIETERICH-WARD, Shippensburg University

—BEVERLY C. TOMEK, University of Houston, Victoria

PENNSYLVANIA HISTORY SERIES EDITORIAL BOARD

JANET LINDMAN, Rowan University

CURT MINER, Pennsylvania Historical and Museum Commission

TRACY NEUMANN, Wayne State University

DONNA RILLING, Stony Brook University

ANNE ROSE, Pennsylvania State University

DANIEL SIDORICK, Rutgers University, New Brunswick

ACKNOWLEDGMENTS

I AM VERY MUCH INDEBTED to Allen Dieterich-Ward, who edited this volume for the *Pennsylvania History Series* and invested considerable time and effort to strengthening the text. I also received thoughtful comments from Beverly C. Tomek, the series co-editor; the anonymous outside readers; and several members of the editorial board. My colleagues Jean Soderlund and Stephen Cutcliffe at Lehigh University each read a chapter and offered valuable suggestions.

A number of librarians provided assistance in arranging for reproductions of the images: Sarah Weatherwax and Nicole Joniec (Library Company), Josue Hurtado (Special Collections, Temple University Libraries), and Laura Stroffolino (Free Library). At Lehigh University, Steven Lichak and Christopher Herrara were immensely helpful in preparing images. Scott A. Drzyzga of Shippensburg University prepared the map included in Chapter 5. The Gipson Institute for Eighteenth-Century Studies and the History Department at Lehigh University provided financial support. The editorial team at Temple University Press was extremely helpful, particularly Debby Smith, who copyedited the manuscript with great care.

Finally, I am enormously grateful to my wife, Marna, who has been incredibly patient and supportive, even going so far as to drive me around old neighborhoods while I took pictures.

INTRODUCTION

PHILADELPHIA'S FOUNDER, William Penn, planned for a "greene Country towne," where detached houses with gardens and orchards would face wide streets and the people would live harmoniously, guided by Quaker principles—it was to be a "holy experiment" and a model community. But Penn had dual motives. He also expected to make a profit on his new colony. Prosperity and community good are not inherently mutually exclusive: a successful community is built on a prosperous one. A sustainable community not only provides a place where people can earn a living but also, through governmental and voluntary efforts, educates the young, facilitates commerce, protects public health, safeguards property and person, offers its citizens access to adequate housing, and provides venues for recreation and cultural expression. Philadelphia's history is the story of the efforts to sustain economic prosperity while fulfilling community needs. It is the story of the circumstances that shaped those efforts and how they shifted over the years. Other cities attempted this balance, but Philadelphia was unique because Penn made explicit his goal of establishing a community that was at once peaceful, attractive, prosperous, and harmonious.

Understanding Philadelphia's history also requires that we understand that nothing is inevitable; history is made not by abstract forces but by the decisions of real individuals as they conduct their lives. Although the options open to citizens can be restrained by the ideas, decisions, and institutions of those who precede them, people have been known to overcome those restraints. At key moments, visionary leaders stepped forward to break with past practices and build new institutions that improved the lives of everyday citizens. Even at the dawn of the twenty-first century, when an impersonal globalization and decisions made beyond their borders appeared to control all change, residents found options that allowed them to take control of their future in important ways. Philadelphians made the city's history.

PHILADELPHIA

1

ESTABLISHING A COMMUNITY/ BUILDING AN ECONOMY

Beginnings to 1800

FROM ITS FIRST SETTLEMENT IN 1682 to the end of the eighteenth century, Philadelphia, and the world around it, changed in profound ways. In the first decade the town was a ramshackle settlement resting precariously on the edge of a vast continent, offering a haven for persecuted English Quakers. By 1750 it was among the largest towns in the British Empire with a port that handled goods from all over the Atlantic basin and attracted thousands of European immigrants. By 1790, with more than forty thousand residents, Philadelphia was the capital city, banking hub, and manufacturing center of a new nation. The settlement patterns, economic functions, civic institutions, and social relationships established in the city's first decades shaped Philadelphia for the next three hundred years.

Economic and Civic Foundations

King Charles II despised Quakers. Their religion challenged the Church of England and their rejection of hierarchy threatened civil order. Persecution in the 1670s had failed to quiet them. But one of their leading spokesmen, William Penn, was well-connected at Court, and the king owed a large debt to Penn's father, who had helped restore Charles to the throne. In the New World the king saw an opportunity to solve two problems at once. In March 1681, to discharge his debt to the family and get rid of the pesky Quakers, he granted Penn a charter to establish a new colony, Pennsylvania (Penn's Woods). Pennsylvania was thus established as a proprietorship that gave Penn and his descendants wide powers to govern the colony. Penn sought to create a model community and a profit-making enterprise, dual purposes that sometimes clashed in the new town established as the hub for his experiment.[1]

At the time, the Delaware Valley was a dense forest with rich soil, great mineral wealth, and favorable growing conditions, but it was not a wilderness. Native people, who called themselves Lenape, had occupied the lower Delaware Valley for untold centuries. In 1600, they lived in small settlements scattered throughout the region where they farmed corn, squash, and beans, hunted game in the forests, and fished in the streams and rivers. They lacked a centralized organization, but village leaders, known as sachems, cooperated with one another. About nine thousand Lenape lived across the region before the arrival of Europeans. By 1681, much diminished by disease, they resided mostly in southern New Jersey. We find their most visible reminder in such place names as Manayunk, Moyamensing, Passyunk, and Shackamaxon.

The distinct attributes of Lenape society and the interactions of the Lenape with the European settlers who drifted into the region between 1615 and 1681 helped to shape Pennsylvania. The native people and the Europeans, mostly from Sweden, Finland, England, and the Netherlands, developed a society of mutual respect, shared use of the land, and peaceful settlement of differences. Their relationship was primarily pragmatic: both sides gained from mutual trade. In 1681, about fifty European families lived within the boundaries of the future Philadelphia, with small clusters at Cobbs Creek, at the mouth of the Schuylkill River, and at Kingsessing, and some Europeans intermarried with the Lenape. The Lenape's peaceful outlook and willingness to sell land to settlers meant that Pennsylvania was the only major colony founded with no threat by Native Americans. It also meant the Quakers could maintain their pacifist ideals and devote resources to private pursuits rather than military defense.[2]

Following Penn's detailed instructions, which laid bare his concern for the commercial aspects of the venture, his agents sited the town at the confluence of two major rivers, the Delaware and the Schuylkill, which would become highways to the interior. An embankment near the Delaware led down to a sandy beach suitable for building wharves out into the water. Numerous creeks ran toward each river, one of which, Dock Creek, fed a small cove off the Delaware that would provide a protected harbor for small craft.

Penn knew that capital and settlers were essential for a successful venture. To attract both, he guaranteed religious toleration—at least for Protestants—and promised limited representative government. Quakers had suffered considerable persecution in Restoration England and had learned from bitter experience that religious freedom and property rights were inextricably linked. If people were not free in their possessions because of their beliefs, then they had no freedom of conscience. Penn therefore wrote basic protections of property and trial by jury into his Frame of Government. He named the principal town Philadelphia, meaning "one who loves his brother." He took the name from an important Greek trading center of the late Hellenic period that was also the location of an early Christian church to which Saint John the Divine addressed a message in the Book of Revelations. Thus the name evoked three potent images: brotherhood, a prosperous port, and Christianity.

Philadelphia began with a town plan. Penn laid out a grid of streets running a mile along the Delaware River waterfront from Vine to South Street and two miles west to the Schuylkill River, for a total of twelve hundred acres. Two wide streets, Market and Broad, divided the town into four sections.* Where those streets crossed, Penn set aside a ten-acre public square (now the site of City Hall). In the middle of each quadrant, Penn reserved eight acres as a public commons (later Franklin, Washington, and Rittenhouse Squares and Logan Circle). The plan conveyed a sense of order and rationality, with open space reserved for public use. In the eighteenth century the squares were, alas, used to dump garbage, hang criminals, and bury the poor. The plan was not entirely original; Penn drew on several English examples, but Philadelphia was the first major American town to be planned. Penn's plan had a determinative effect in shaping the city's growth. Furthermore, as Americans founded new towns across the continent, they repeatedly copied his plan.

Penn wanted Philadelphia to avoid the congestion of London, which suffered an outbreak of bubonic plague in 1665 and a disastrous fire in 1666. He therefore provided for large square blocks with generous house lots. Penn expected that houses would be located in the middle of the plots, keeping the density low. In a rapidly growing commercial port, however, everyone sought to be as close to the waterfront as possible, so as early as the 1690s owners subdivided lots and cut through narrow alleys. Despite Penn's hopes for a "greene Country towne," Philadelphia quickly became a dense urban place with substantial houses facing the main streets but with cramped houses squeezed into narrow alleys and courts where artisans plied their craft in their front room and lived above. In the trade-off between community and commerce, commerce was winning out.[3]

---

*The names of many Center City streets have changed. For example, the original name of Market Street was High, Race Street was Sassafras, Arch Street was Mulberry, and South Street was Cedar. To avoid confusion, I use current names throughout.

Word of Penn's experiment generated enormous excitement, especially among Quakers, who, like the New England Puritans, placed a strong emphasis on self-discipline and self-control: hard work was a virtue and a duty, idleness a waste of God's resources. Developing God's bounty was one's duty, and if doing so led to improvement in one's material position, it was a positive sign that one was doing God's work. Because of this mix of Puritan self-discipline with religious democracy, Quakerism appealed particularly to market-oriented people with entrepreneurial skills. Quakers flocked to the colony along with Presbyterians, Anglicans, and Baptists from England, Scotland, Wales, Ireland, and Germany. Most people took up farms in the countryside, but within a decade the town's population surpassed two thousand. Africans were also among the town's earliest residents, but they were involuntary immigrants: the first slave ship arrived to sell its human cargo in 1684. Penn also granted land to a group of German pietists; their village along the Wissahickon Creek, six miles from Philadelphia, became known as "Germantown."

By 1700, Philadelphia was taking the shape and appearance that would characterize it throughout the eighteenth century. Settlement spread in a thin ribbon along the Delaware waterfront, extending west only a few blocks. More than a hundred shops and warehouses crowded between Front Street and the riverbank. One could walk from one end of town to the other in half an hour. Although most houses were timber frame, abundant nearby clay and limestone made bricks inexpensive and brick town houses would eventually dominate, providing a decidedly urbane appearance. The Swedes erected a substantial church, Gloria Dei (Old Swedes Church), which has stood for three hundred years, and the Quakers built a fifty-foot-square meeting house at Second and Market Streets.

To maintain their living standards, Pennsylvanians needed English manufactured goods, such as pots, kettles, tools, axes, rifles, gunpowder and shot, cloth, glass, paper, books, and furnishings. But, except for deerskins and other furs, England had little need for Pennsylvania's products. To prosper, Philadelphia merchants had to find markets for the region's abundant agricultural surplus to pay for their imports. Thus, the success of the town and the region were intertwined. As the colony grew, so did the town, which reached ten thousand by 1740; twenty years later, with more than eighteen thousand residents, Philadelphia had displaced Boston as the largest town in the colonies. At the outbreak of the Revolution it was the fourth largest town in the British Empire.

Philadelphia attracted many Quaker merchants, who arrived with established contacts in other Atlantic ports, accumulated capital, good reputations, and entrepreneurial skill, positioning the town to compete with older and larger rivals. Philadelphia was closer to the Caribbean than Boston or New

York, and its merchants sent south the produce that fed African slaves on sugar plantations. Returning ships carried rum, coffee, molasses, enslaved humans, and, most important, currency to pay for goods Philadelphia imported from Britain. In the eighteenth century, merchants also opened lucrative markets with Spain, Portugal, Madeira, and the Canary Islands. In addition, a thriving commerce developed with the other colonial ports, and by the time the American Revolution began, Philadelphia had become a major supplier of foodstuffs to New England.

Colonial Philadelphia had a remarkably complex economy, with as many trades as could be found in a much larger town. The port stood at the core, directly or indirectly employing most of the people. Longshoremen (often African slaves) loaded and unloaded vessels and moved goods through the streets. Along the waterfront more than a dozen shipyards kept busy hundreds of skilled craftsmen—together with apprentices, laborers, and slaves—building ships and making sails, barrels, rope, and tackle. Distilleries, breweries, tanneries, and slaughterhouses clustered along Dock Creek. Carpenters and bricklayers built houses for a rapidly growing population. Printers supplied legal and business documents and published two weekly newspapers that announced auctions and published commodity prices and shipping information in addition to local and international news. Beyond the town, water-powered mills along the Wissahickon Creek made the village of Germantown an important processing center for agricultural produce. Colonial merchants also invested their profits in the region's development, especially in Delaware Valley iron forges, making the region a major center of North American iron production. By the eve of the Revolution, iron was a valuable export sent directly to England. In those ways the accumulated profits of the port of Philadelphia contributed to the development and diversification of the entire region.[4]

In contrast to the town's successful economic growth, the municipal government, the Corporation of Philadelphia, was a conspicuous failure. From the beginning a narrow elite of wealthy landowners and merchants controlled the Corporation. When it came to encouraging commerce, the aldermen showed considerable initiative, building and maintaining public docks and the finest public markets in the colonies, but on matters dealing with health and communal well-being, the Corporation was remarkably sluggish and unresponsive. The initiative to address problems came from civic-minded men who organized as volunteers or petitioned the Pennsylvania Assembly to widen the scope of public responsibility. Their achievements made Philadelphia a model for other colonial towns to follow.[5]

Like other colonial ports, Philadelphia in the eighteenth century was a dangerous place to live, although much less so than any English town. The

Arch Street Ferry, Delaware River Waterfront, 1799, an engraving by William Birch, provides a sanitized view of the activity along the busy waterfront (without the garbage, trash, and horse and pig manure that coated the streets). To the left and in the lower left and right corners, boys and men load heavy barrels and crates onto carts. (William Russell Birch and the Library Company of Philadelphia.)

death rate was appalling. A fifth to a quarter of all babies died before age five, and childbirth took the lives of many women. People who survived to twenty-one rarely reached age sixty. Chronic maladies, such as tuberculosis, diphtheria, measles, whooping cough, and venereal disease took a heavy toll every year, although the periodic epidemics, such as smallpox, were more frightening in their virulence. Smallpox inoculation, which became widespread late in the century, helped reduce the mortality rate. As with so many other aspects of life, inoculation was problematic for the poor. It was not free, and the patient had to rest for days, a burden for those who lived from day to day.[6]

Since no one knew the causes of disease, people drank from communal cups, and they did not much bother to wash their hands, bodies, or clothes. Residents dumped their kitchen waste in the streets, where it mixed with the abundant manure of horses, dogs, and pigs. Outdoor privies were dangerously close to backyard pumps. By the late 1730s, Dock Creek was an open sewer. The eight tanneries and various distilleries, breweries, and slaughterhouses that lined its banks and tributaries all dumped their refuse into the waterway. It was also a cheap and convenient place in which to dispose of dead animals, which floated slowly down to the Delaware, mixing with raw sewage en route and emitting a dreadful odor. Although no one could demonstrate a direct connection between polluted water and disease, people intuitively understood what they could not prove and complained frequently of the putrid stench. A rash of epidemics led to a concerted effort to clean up the creek, and in 1739 a petition to the colonial assembly called for relocation of the noxious uses to a more remote site. But nothing changed. Beginning in the 1760s, the Corporation covered over Dock Creek in several stages. This action was a sensible response to the open sewer, but it ignored the alternative of careful protection of the water supply and segregation of necessary but adverse land uses in the name of unrestricted property rights. Philadelphia continued to pollute its waterways shamelessly and recklessly for another two hundred years.[7]

Fire, like disease, was a constant danger, and fire-fighting techniques were primitive and consisted mostly of calling out nearby residents to toss buckets of water on the burning structure. Occasionally, in the chaos of the moment, some residents would help themselves to unguarded household goods and

Southeast Corner of Third and Market Streets, 1799, an engraving by William Birch, shows the range of activities conducted in these streets lined by substantial brick buildings. At left are meat stalls, and at the intersection a butcher carves a side of beef. Native Americans and African Americans form part of the street scene. No unkempt individuals are in view. (William Birch & Son and the Library Company of Philadelphia.)

merchandise. After a serious conflagration in 1730 destroyed a wharf and several warehouses, the Corporation acquired new buckets and a pumping engine, but it rejected efforts to regulate chimney cleaning and made no effort to improve firefighting or prevent looting. Thus, in 1736, a group of artisans organized the volunteer Union Fire Company. The idea, borrowed from Boston, caught on more rapidly in Philadelphia, perhaps because of the laxity of the local government, and other volunteer companies followed. Protection of property was always important to the middling sort, and the civic-mindedness of the men who volunteered to protect property (mostly each other's) reflected a growing public awareness of the interdependence of the urban community.

In other areas, the community did much better. For decades, citizens complained about the wretched conditions of the streets. A 1739 report labeled Arch and Vine open sewers. The drawbridge over Dock Creek was often in disrepair, causing considerable inconvenience. A night watch was organized to patrol the dark streets, keeping a lookout for fires and thieves, but citizens so often shirked this unpaid obligation that the watch had little effect. At midcentury the colonial assembly, sidestepping the Corporation, established separate special-purpose elected boards with taxing powers and responsibility for paving, drainage, street lighting, and a paid night watch. Those acts recognized that the urban habitat was a communal responsibility and that personal safety and protection of property required public revenue. Philadelphia soon acquired a reputation for clean, well-paved, and well-lighted streets. The main streets, however, benefited the most; the numerous alleys, lanes, and courts of the laboring people and poor often remained dark, dirty, and unpaved.

It is not surprising that, as the colonies' largest town, Philadelphia pioneered such projects, but it is extraordinary that one man, Benjamin Franklin, was involved in virtually every civic initiative from the 1730s through the 1750s. Franklin possessed tremendous natural talent—intelligence, imagination, practicality, and personal charm. He learned the printing trade from his older brother but left his native Boston at age sixteen to strike out on his own. Shortly after his arrival in Philadelphia, he went to London, where he spent eighteen months as a journeyman printer, a unique experience for a young colonist in the 1720s. Back in Philadelphia Franklin started a weekly newspaper, the *Pennsylvania Gazette,* which he quickly made the most influential newspaper in town and later in the colonies. His *Poor Richard's Almanac* was second only to the Bible in popularity among colonial readers.

In a stunning range of endeavors, Franklin led the citizenry to understand the obligations of civic life and the importance of creating a livable environment. Further, he consistently advanced an ethos of democratic self-improvement. He espoused the Protestant work ethic of his Boston background but without the religious doctrine. In 1727, only twenty-one years old, he formed a discussion group with other like-minded and ambitious young artisans, the Club of the Leather Apron Men, known as the Junto. From Franklin and his Junto soon tumbled a host of proposals for improving the town. In 1731 they organized the Library Company, a private circulating collection. Subscribed to by fifty young tradesmen, it provided an opportunity for ambitious "middling people" to learn of the ideas and intellectual currents of contemporary Europe. It was a remarkably democratic institution for self-advancement. In 1747, when the city feared attack from the French, Franklin hastily organized voluntary militia companies in which the men elected their own officers, reflecting his strongly egalitarian outlook.

Franklin played the leading role in founding the Pennsylvania Hospital for the Sick Poor, the College of Philadelphia (later the University of Pennsylvania), and the American Philosophical Society, the nation's oldest learned society. Pennsylvania Hospital, which pioneered in humane treatment of the mentally ill, was the first hospital in the British colonies. The college was the first in the colonies not founded primarily to train clergymen, and, in 1765, it established the colonies' first medical school, laying the basis for the city's preeminence in medical education in the following century. Most of Franklin's initiatives did not involve the government; they were private, volunteer, and democratic.[8]

Class, Race, and Daily Life in a Colonial Town

People knew their social place in the eighteenth century, when distinctions were marked not just by wealth and occupation but also by clothes, manners, forms of address, and habits of deference, as well as by gender and race. Quakers believe all are equal in God's eyes, but the Quakers in Philadelphia certainly embraced differences in rank and status, weakening any true sense of community that Penn might have hoped for. Colonial Philadelphians can be divided roughly into three main groups, known in contemporary terms as the "better sort," the "middling sort," and the "lower sort." As the city became more diverse and cosmopolitan, race, gender, and condition of servitude also shaped the rhythms of urban life.

The better sort, a small elite of wealthy merchants and substantial landowners, provincial officials, and successful professionals—doctors, lawyers, clergy—dominated the town and the colony. Quakers were overrepresented among this upper group that at most accounted for 10 percent of the people but, by 1760, owned about two-thirds of the personal wealth. Members of the upper group were part of an international network of ideas and culture nourished by contacts in ports throughout the Atlantic World. They lived in sub-

Second Street North from Market Street, 1799, an engraving by William Birch, shows the center of Market Street, with the old City Hall at the left. Women sit in front displaying their wares, and an African American woman carries a basket of laundry on her head. In the lower left corner, a man standing in a cart sells chickens. An African American boy holding a basket crosses the street. Above the houses rises the steeple of Christ Church (Anglican). (William Russell Birch and the Library Company of Philadelphia.)

stantial houses in the center of town, away from the odors of the waterfront and markets, notably along Chestnut, Walnut, Pine, and Locust between Second and Third Streets. They imported fine-quality English furniture, ate on bone china with sterling silver, drank the best wines, covered their tables, chairs, and beds in the finest fabrics, and rode about in carriages. The elegance of the colonial gentry can still be glimpsed at the Powel House on Third Street and in a cluster of surviving country houses along the banks of the Schuylkill River in Fairmount Park.[9]

Among all social groups, women derived their status from that of their fathers or husbands. Wealthy women were literate and often kept up with political affairs. They managed complex households that included servant girls and house slaves. Typical of such women was Elizabeth Drinker, whose father and husband were wealthy Quaker merchants. Drinker received an education unusual for her time and left a remarkable diary. Her concerns were mostly those of private family life, and her tribulations were similar to those of parents at all times. Well versed in medical knowledge of the day, she was a nurse and caregiver to family and friends, and she managed to hold her family together when her husband, Henry, was arrested for his pacifism during the Revolution. Later in the century their home became a refuge for runaway slaves, although Elizabeth never overcame her condescension toward blacks.[10]

The middling sort—shopkeepers, master artisans, small-scale merchants, and professionals of modest means—enjoyed a measure of respectability and social standing, particularly the shopkeepers and lesser merchants who advanced credit to their customers. The master craftsmen ran their own workshops with the help, at most, of a few journeymen and apprentices and perhaps a slave. Journeymen, younger artisans who lacked the capital to set up on their own, filled the ranks of the lower end of the group. Unmarried journeymen usually lived in the master artisan's house. Men of the middling sort could vote, and they took politics seriously; they held the minor offices that might advance their standing. Their small houses usually had a store or workshop in the front room. They could afford simple but adequate furniture: beds, a dining table and chairs, a few chests. Around midcentury, as the town became more prosperous, these families acquired more material possessions. When Benjamin Franklin's wife wanted china and silver to replace their earthenware and pewter, she wanted it "to be as good as [the] neighbors."[11]

Like those above them, middling women managed complex households. While they often had servants or slaves, wives and daughters did much of the housework themselves and they might also help their husbands run a shop or business. Some widows who inherited a retail store or a tavern could be counted among the middling sort. Others ran boarding houses or worked as nurses or midwives, although the pay was low. A few educated women taught or gave music or language lessons, but most women had few opportunities for respectable employment. The house and furnishings of John and Betsy Ross on Arch Street provide a surviving example of a home of the middling people.[12]

Two distinct groups formed the lower sort: workers with little or no skill and dependents whose freedom was restricted. The free people of the lower sort filled the ranks of lesser skilled occupations. Some worked as tailors, shoemakers, and coopers, but most toiled as porters, longshoremen, woodcutters, ditch diggers, common seamen, or day laborers. Accounting for almost half of the workforce, they owned few possessions and lived in cramped, rented quarters usually near the docks and toward the edges of town. A cluster could be found in the neighborhood aptly labeled "Helltown," just north of Arch Street, east of Third Street. Observers sometimes described the accommodations of the poorest as "huts," "sheds," and "mean, low boxes of wood." In such foul and congested alleys and courts, where residents survived on inadequate diets and lacked warm clothing, disease found a congenial environment and took a heavy toll. The town's outward prosperity did not trickle down to them.

The women and children of the lower sort also worked. Wives and daughters might supplement income by taking in boarders or laundry, or doing domestic work for the better sort. They did the town's heavy and unpleasant housework: scrubbing floors, emptying chamber pots, and cooking over fireplaces. Widows and adult single women on their own struggled to survive. A few operated retail shops or taverns and had a toehold among the middling sort, but most ranked among the poor. Some took in sewing or peddled goods in the streets. Desperate young women without skills or family might turn to prostitution, which was widespread in a port with numerous transients and sailors. Children could scavenge for wood, peddle goods, or sweep chimneys.[13]

Dependents with restricted freedom included apprentices, indentured servants, and slaves. Apprentices, mostly teenage boys, lived in their master's house, subject to his rules and discipline while learning a trade or skill. Philadelphia also had a substantial number of indentured servants, most of whom were Irish, Scotch-Irish, or German immigrants in their teens and early twenties. They had sold their labor, usually for four to seven years, to pay off their passage: women as domestics, men as laborers. According to the indenture agreement, they were to be taught reading and writing but not any particular skill. Poor families sometimes indentured their own children if they could not support them. Also, the overseers of the poor frequently indentured orphans and children of parents seeking public relief, sometimes at a young age, and sometimes against their parents' will. Indentured servants had fewer rights or protections than apprentices. Frequent reports of runaways suggest that exploitation and abuse were common.[14]

Those in need of charity or public relief constituted the indigent poor. Most were women, especially single women, impoverished because of pregnancy, childcare responsibilities, low wages, widowhood, and old age. With a jump in population around midcentury, the poor increasingly appeared threatening. Wandering the streets begging, they were viewed as potential thieves and prostitutes. The authorities described them as "worthless," "undeserving," or "vicious" people who might need aid but also supervision. Thus, aid was kept stingy and degrading in an effort to encourage work and keep the tax burden low. In 1767, Philadelphia opened the Bettering House, a combination almshouse and workhouse. The largest building in British North America, it suggested a strong civic commitment to aid the distressed, but the reality was more complex. The initiative came from wealthy merchants who wanted the able-bodied poor to be taught discipline and some skill, and then put to work. Because those merchants saw the principal cause of poverty to be a defect of character, the intent was more reform than charity. The scheme represented an extraordinary mix of public and private authority: a board of managers elected by only wealthy contributors ran it. The managers expected that relief given to the needy in their homes would cease, although the overseers of the poor resisted. They were elected officials, usually of the middling sort, who were just a little closer to those in need than the Bettering House managers. The overseers saw the Bettering House for what it was: incarceration for the crime of being poor.[15]

From the outset there were African slaves in Philadelphia, as there were in every other northern colony. During the eighteenth century, slavery in Philadelphia fluctuated in accordance with the availability of indentured servants. Slaves peaked as a share of the town's population at about 17 percent around 1710, but in absolute numbers the peak came in the 1760s, when fourteen hundred slaves comprised 8 percent of the total population. In the 1760s about 20 percent of households owned a slave. In 1773, Pennsylvania largely ended the slave trade by taxing slave importation, and by 1775 the number and percentage of slaves had fallen sharply.

Constituting, in the 1760s, about 20 percent of the laborers along the docks, the men performed a considerable fraction of the city's backbreaking work; most female slaves were domestics. Although the work and living conditions of slaves in Philadelphia were less harsh than in the plantation South, the frequency of runaway notices, as well as the occasional suicide and homicide, revealed their cruelty. In Philadelphia, whites who owned only one or two slaves lived in intimate contact with their slaves and worked alongside them.

Economic necessity and the density of the town enabled African Americans far greater freedom of movement than those in rural areas. Gradually they were able to define spaces for social gatherings. Early in the century, the town had set aside a separate black burial ground that became a regular meeting place, as did the space in front of the courthouse on Sundays. With some semblance of family life and a regular place to meet, black people were able to perpetuate elements of their African culture. A small free black community began to emerge in the middle decades and grew rapidly just before the Revolution, when they numbered between four hundred and six hundred, about 20 percent of the total black population.[16]

For all races and classes, the patterns of daily life in the pre-industrial age varied greatly from that of modern times. People lived, worked, shopped, and worshipped within small areas, and although there was always a transient population, each neighborhood contained dense networks of family and friends. People bought their food from street venders, who were usually women and children, or at the thrice-weekly farmers' stalls that lined the center of Market Street and later in Southwark and Northern Liberties. Recreational and leisure outlets were limited and often revolved around alcohol. Workers expected to drink on the job and might consume two to three quarts of beer a day. This practice may have contributed to the numerous accidents at job sites. Much of the town's social life occurred in the ubiquitous taverns, and virtually all free men, and many women, frequented them. At first, gentlemen and journeymen often sat around one large table, fostering a rough egalitarianism in the customs of treating one another to a round, toasting friends, singing together, and debating political developments.

By the middle of the eighteenth century, the town became more cosmopolitan and the classes began to go their separate ways. Several coffeehouses catered to merchants and served as informal exchanges for commercial news and business dealings. Theaters, notably the Walnut Street Theater, offered plays for the better off, while elsewhere wagering on cockfights and horse races provided amusement. All the entertainments involved drinking and usually sexual license, as the rapidly growing and heterogeneous town encouraged a degree of toleration not found elsewhere.[17]

The colony's reputation for toleration also encouraged religious dissenters. By midcentury, German Reformed, Lutheran, Moravian, Baptist, and Presbyterian churches abounded. Anglicans erected the imposing Georgian-style Christ Church at Second and Arch Streets where many of the Founding Fathers prayed. The modest St. Joseph's Chapel for Roman Catholics arose in Willing's Alley near Fourth Street, where the fourth structure still stands on the site. Sephardic Jews established a congregation in the 1740s and erected Mikveh Israel on Cherry Street in 1782. An evangelical movement known as the Great Awakening swept through the colonies in the 1740s, offering the democratic promise of salvation to those who embraced Christ. Its leading advocate, the charismatic George Whitefield, preached to a reported fifteen thousand people at an open-air meeting in 1740. He was so persuasive that even the skeptical Benjamin Franklin emptied his purse into the collection plate and later reported that Whitefield, temporarily at least, increased piety in Philadelphia.

Slowly white Philadelphia awoke to the horrors of slavery. In 1754, the Quaker Meeting condemned the practice as a sin. In 1774, Quakers took a stronger stand and pressured its members to free their slaves, and two years later, decided to disown any Friend who engaged in the slave trade or continued to own slaves. Although Quakers made a strong commitment to antislavery after the Revolution, they were never too eager to welcome blacks into their ranks. Anglicans were more receptive: Christ Church baptized and married several black couples. Anglicans and Quakers sponsored free schools for black children before the Revolution. Only the Quakers, however, showed much interest in the actual conditions of free blacks.[18]

In 1780, Pennsylvania passed a law that provided for the gradual abolition of slavery. Although it was the first abolition law in any Western nation, it did not immediately free any slaves. Children of slaves born after 1780 would gain freedom at age twenty-eight. Despite the gradual aspect of the law, Philadelphia quickly became a magnet for newly freed slaves and runaways, and many owners conformed to the spirit of the law by releasing slaves born before 1780 when they reached about age twenty-eight. In 1783, the town housed about four hundred slaves and a thousand free blacks; in 1800, fifty-five remained enslaved alongside six thousand free blacks. Thirty years later, thirteen slaves lived in the city proper. Free blacks filled the ranks of the least desirable and lowest-paying jobs and were overrepresented in the almshouse. A very few became artisans and petty proprietors.[19]

By the dawn of the new century Philadelphia would emerge as the center of free black culture in America. In 1787, two African American preachers, Richard Allen, a former slave, and Absalom Jones, founded the Free African Society, the country's first independent black institution, which aided free blacks and held religious services. In the 1790s, the African American community established two autonomous churches where, free of patronizing and hostile whites, they could find solidarity for their woes and an emotional outlet for their feelings. Jones founded the African Episcopal Church of St. Thomas on Fifth Street near Spruce, the nation's first free black congregation, while Allen organized the Bethel African Methodist Episcopal Church (later known as Mother Bethel) on Sixth Street between Pine and Lombard. The churches quickly became cultural and social centers and sponsored schools for the children.

From Port City to National Capital

The events leading up to the American Revolution involved two overlapping yet distinct struggles that unfolded simultaneously. The first was the conflict between the colonies and the British government; the second was a struggle over political participation within Pennsylvania. Although a majority of white male adults met the property qualification for voting, the Proprietor and his appointed council continued to run the colony. By the 1760s this imbalance in power caused considerable discord. In 1765, Parliament imposed a direct tax on Americans for the first time with the Stamp Act. In the protests that followed, no one was tarred and feathered, but only because a crowd of eight hundred persuaded the appointed stamp collector to resign the post. Philadelphia merchants, already facing weakened trade, lined up behind a boycott of British goods in protest. In 1768, however, when other ports renewed the boycott to protest the Townshend Act duties, local merchants refused to participate. Artisans and mechanics had to pressure them for a full year to support a renewed boycott. In 1770, the leading merchants attempted to drop nonimportation and told the artisans they were "rabble," with no right to express their views on matters of trade. This rebuke galvanized into action men of the middling sort, who feared that British trade policy was slowly narrowing their options and opportunities.

Public sentiment was articulated in the newspapers, in taverns, and at street meetings and rallies, usually held at the State House yard. Such gatherings were more democratic than the Pennsylvania Assembly, since many voices could be heard, and even the disenfranchised—propertyless men, women, and servants—could shout out their support. Protest leaders used rallies to show merchants they had broad support. At a May 1770 public meeting a group of artisans established the Mechanics Committee, which began to function as a political party. Artisans soon won election to minor local and county offices. In the fall, voters elected a tradesman to the assembly for the first time in the eighteenth century. The artisans' agenda focused more on issues of power at home than on struggles with Parliament. For the first time, assembly debates and roll calls were published in full, and a public gallery was erected in the State House.[20]

Over the next several years Philadelphia's artisans, supported by the lower orders, gained in strength and influence. The Anglican and Quaker elite merchants' hesitation to support the revolutionary cause provided an opening. In 1775, in open elections for a committee to enforce the boycott protesting the Intolerable Acts, British laws punishing Massachusetts for the Boston Tea Party of 1773, the artisans and their allies defeated the merchants and took full control of the revolutionary movement. As a result, in 1776 Pennsylvania adopted the most democratic constitution of any state, giving all male taxpayers the franchise. It provided for annual elections to the assembly and abolished the elitist City Corporation. The influence of the merchants, many of whom became Loyalists, or, as Quakers, attempted to remain neutral, went into eclipse.

When, in response to the Intolerable Acts, Bostonians called on the other colonies to send delegates to a continent-wide congress, Philadelphia, as the largest and most centrally located port, was the logical site. The First Continental Congress met in September 1775 at Carpenters' Hall between Fifth and Sixth Streets, where it took steps to coordinate a boycott on British goods. The following May, the Second Continental Congress convened at the State House, where, on July 4, 1776, delegates signed the Declaration of Independence. Philadelphia was now the nation's capital.

The Revolution brought economic and social upheaval. In March 1776, the British blockaded the Delaware River, closing the port and throwing thousands out of work. Local manufacture of uniforms and war materiel, however, propped up employment for another year. In September 1777, British troops occupied Philadelphia. Since its capture was expected, there was ample time to remove virtually all usable war materiel as well as the State House bell (later known as the Liberty Bell). Most of the able-bodied adult male residents fled along with the Congress. When the Redcoats arrived, more than 10 percent of the houses stood vacant. But the population soon swelled as the occupied town attracted Loyalists, deserters, and runaway slaves. Although the British army pumped some money into the local economy, overall the town suffered badly under the occupation. Estimates placed the combined loss from property damage, theft, and vandalism at £187,000. Further, Loyalist sympathizers intensified social divisions laid bare during the revolutionary crisis by hosting lavish parties for the British troops. When the British departed on June 18, 1778, about three thousand Loyalists and dozens of slaves fled with them. They left behind lingering animosities.

The worst years of the war came after the British left. The port remained closed and the economy stagnant. Congress, struggling to finance the war, simply printed money, fueling inflation. The hardships exacerbated conflict between the populace and the merchants, even those who supported the Revolution. In 1779, the tension finally burst open in the worst civil disturbance Philadelphia had yet seen. As inflation spiraled out of control, working people, with good reason, suspected merchants of holding back grain for a higher price. In January, sailors striking for higher wages broke apart some ships and started a small riot. In April, the assembly required sellers to accept inflated paper currency. In May, a public meeting appointed a committee to set prices on basic commodities, but this action only aggravated the situation because farmers refused to bring grain to market for fear they might be forced to sell below cost. Although the summer crop was good, the shortage of grain persisted; meanwhile trade was at a standstill. Accusations flew back and forth between the radical and moderate factions.

On October 4, 1779, a mob attempted to seize James Wilson, a leading merchant and signer of the Declaration of Independence who was suspected of profiteering. Wilson and his supporters barricaded themselves in his fashionable house at Third and Walnut. When the mob rushed the house they were greeted with a volley of gunfire and a short battle ensued. Five men died and seventeen were wounded in what became known as the Fort Wilson riot. The attack broke some of the tension, as both sides shrank back from greater violence, but it revealed the extent to which the Revolution had eroded the social equilibrium of colonial Philadelphia.[21]

The end of the war in 1783 brought continued economic dislocation and a severe depression. The British West Indies were now closed to American ships, but merchants opened new markets with the French, Dutch, and Spanish islands, the European continent, and Asia. Nonetheless, trade languished through the rest of the decade. By the mid-1780s the merchant community was regaining its standing because the populace hoped it would restore prosperity. Meanwhile a conservative faction worked to establish a stronger federal government and to roll back the most democratic features of the 1776 state constitution. Although Congress had moved to New York in 1783, in the summer of 1787 delegates from twelve states convened at the State House to draft a new frame of government. It was brutally hot, but the men inside kept the windows closed to avoid premature disclosure of their deliberations.

After sweating through numerous historic compromises, delegates signed the Constitution on September 17; Benjamin Franklin, indefatigable at age eighty-one, was among them. Almost a year later, on July 4, 1788, Philadelphia celebrated ratification with the Grand Federal Procession, one of the largest parades in its history. Accompanied by numerous bands, more than five thousand people marched in militia companies and under the banners of their trade or craft, pulling floats through the streets. The large crowd, estimated at seventeen thousand, affirmed civic pride, national patriotism, and democratic participation.[22]

In the 1790s Philadelphia once again served as the national capital. The new Bank of the United States, housed in a handsome classical building on Third Street below Chestnut, confirmed Philadelphia as the country's banking center. Most important, commerce revived. Europe was at war for most of the decade, providing an eager market for Pennsylvania grain and oppor-

---

Facing page: This 1794 map shows the street plan of Philadelphia and, in the shaded area, the region settled by the 1790s. Notice how the population hugged the waterfront, expanding into Southwark and Northern Liberties. (Peter C. Varle and the Library Company of Philadelphia.)

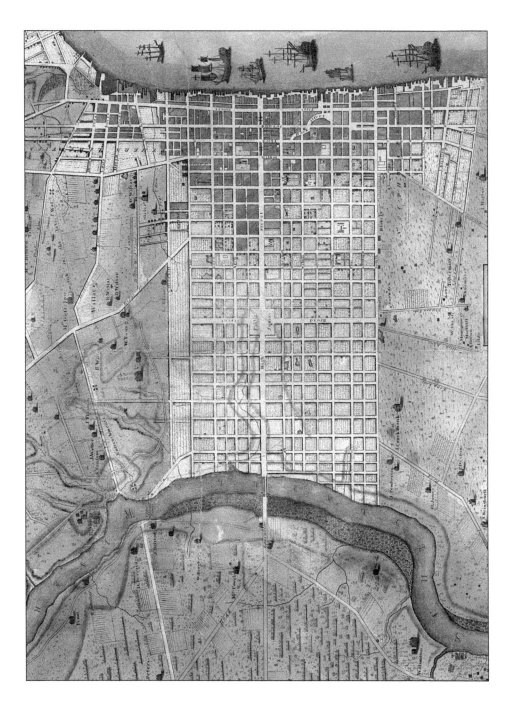

tunities for carrying the commodities of belligerent nations. Those developments brought large profits to the merchants and employment along the docks and shipyards. The boom fueled a 40 percent jump in population to 61,559 in 1800, as the resurgent economy attracted domestic and foreign migrants. The number of houses jumped 60 percent. (New York's population, however, soared by 83 percent to pull even with the Quaker city.) Many immigrants were Irish weavers displaced by mechanization and hoping to carry on their trade in America. Settlement spilled beyond the original city limits, spreading in a thin ribbon about two miles along the Delaware waterfront but, except near the center, no farther west than Sixth Street.

During the decade, wealthy merchants built large townhouses and elegant country estates, but ordinary workers saw little improvement. Journeymen artisans, especially those in the construction and furniture trades, as well as shoemakers and printers, sensing that the opportunities for upward mobility were limited, began to organize separately from their employers. Their societies provided mutual insurance funds, possibly to keep them independent of public charities, and initiated some informal negotiations with employers. In 1796, printers appear to have engaged in the first work stoppage over piece rates.[23]

The social antagonisms of the Revolutionary era partly receded, largely in a victory for the conservative elements who succeeded in revising the state constitution and reimposing a property requirement for voting. The assembly finally granted a new city charter, creating a complex government that reflected the more conservative mood. The city council consisted of fifteen aldermen and thirty common councilmen. All free men voted for the common council, but only property owners elected the aldermen, who, in turn, selected the mayor from among their ranks. A county courthouse and a city hall arose on either side of the State House, just in time to serve as Supreme Court chamber and Congress Hall for the national government.[24]

As the nation's capital, Philadelphia saw firsthand the political factions emerging over such issues as the nation's debt and a national bank. President George Washington and Secretary of the Treasury Alexander Hamilton pushed measures that strengthened the national government and promoted business interests, while Secretary of State Thomas Jefferson and his congressional ally James Madison led the opposition. The Hamiltonians called themselves Federalists; their opponents took the name Democratic-Republicans. As partisanship grew heated, ordinary people took part in the drama of national politics. Civic occasions, especially the July Fourth celebration, found each faction rallying its supporters. The public reading of the Declaration of Independence and other rituals, such as parades and competing open-air feasts with sponsors raising toasts to their leaders, allowed common folk to participate in shaping political institutions at a time when not all citizens could vote. Such events and symbols, extensively reported in the newspapers, were widely emulated across the country.[25]

After years of neglect, the new local government invested in street and infrastructure improvements, but public health remained as precarious as ever. In 1793, a yellow fever epidemic swept through town. It was the most frightening and deadly epidemic the city would ever see. Within four months upwards of five thousand people died, 10 percent of the entire population. A convergence of several factors explains the outbreak. Yellow fever is spread by the *Aedes aegypti* mosquito, usually confined to the tropics. Like all mosquitos, they breed in stagnant water. It rained heavily in the spring of 1793, leaving puddles in the streets. In addition, almost every yard had a rain barrel, and no one had window screens. In the same year some two thousand refugees, fleeing the slave revolt on the French island of Saint-Dominque (Haiti), crowded into town, bringing both the virus and the mosquitos with them.

Panic swept Philadelphia. As the disease spread, almost half the population fled, which was actually an effective response, since the mosquitos did not travel far. People camped in tents around the periphery as virtually all economic activity came to a standstill. The federal government shifted some offices to Germantown. Those left behind, for the most part, lacked the resources to flee, so laborers and the poor accounted for most of the deaths. Organized government collapsed and with it any attempt to aid the sick. Victims were taken to Bush Hill, a country home just north of the city. It became a vile pest house until two private citizens came forward and took charge: Stephen Girard, a merchant from the French West Indies, and Peter Helm, a barrel maker. Girard brought in French refugee doctors who had some experience with the disease; they saved some lives and eased the agonies of many others. They had help from a number of African American volunteers. At first blacks appeared immune to yellow fever. Those with a Caribbean background probably had acquired immunity. By later in the fall, however, blacks too were falling victim.

Three milder outbreaks occurred during the next four years, but an epidemic in 1798 was as virulent as the first, and almost everyone scattered into the countryside. Yellow fever had devastated Philadelphia periodically since its founding, but the epidemics of the 1790s were exceptionally frightening and revealed the human costs of neglecting public needs. In twelve years more than ten thousand died from yellow fever.[26]

———————

BY THE 1790s, Philadelphia was a major Atlantic port, the political and financial capital of a new nation, and a diverse community. Sustaining economic prosperity was the first priority, but Philadelphians demonstrated a remarkable spirit of public responsibility. Visionary leaders such as Benjamin Franklin suggested solutions to urban problems and proposed a host of institutions to enrich everyday life, but progress also required citizens willing to embrace the leaders' vision. As a town was becoming a city, Philadelphians were making their own history.

2

COMMUNITY GOOD/
MANUFACTURING CITY

1800–1865

IN THE FIRST HALF of the nineteenth century, the population of Philadelphia*
exploded from 68,000 to more than 350,000 and then jumped to 566,000 by
1860, making it the world's fourth largest city after London, Paris, and New
York. Industrialization, immigration, and political democracy transformed the
way people lived, worked, and related to one another. Forward-looking political
and civic leaders developed the public-sector infrastructure vital to sustaining a large population while entrepreneurs and businessmen invested in new
technologies that provided opportunities for thousands. New York and Boston
experienced similar transformations, but in important ways Philadelphia led
the nation in embracing the responsibilities of a large city.

Industrialization and Urban Growth

Early in the new century Philadelphia's dominance in foreign trade slipped
away. After the Revolution the British excluded American ships from the
West Indies colonies that had been so important in the eighteenth century.
New markets opened in continental Europe, China, and South America;

---

*From 1682 until 1854, the City of Philadelphia remained confined to the original boundaries
of Vine to South Street between the two rivers, even as the population spread far beyond those
boundaries. In this chapter, I use the term "city proper" to refer to this municipality and "the
city council" or "the mayor" to refer to its government. "Philadelphia," "Philadelphians," and
"the city" refer to the entire built-up area and its people. In references after 1854, these terms
refer to the boundaries of the present city and its government.

The Delaware waterfront of the nineteenth century was lined with the masts of sailing ships. This 1860s view of the wharf of Patterson and Lippincott Lumber Merchants at the foot of Popular Street shows ships sailing behind the piles of lumber along the docks. (Frederick Gutekunst and the Library Company of Philadelphia.)

New York, however, was better situated to capture that trade and by 1810 became the nation's largest city. Philadelphia's port continued to thrive as the number of vessels arriving from other U.S. cities jumped from one thousand in 1815 to more than ten thousand in the mid-1830s and more than twenty-five thousand by 1850, but the source of dynamic growth had to be found elsewhere. Philadelphia merchants looked westward to tap the region's rapidly growing hinterland as a market for the city's output. Early in the new century the city's promoters financed a network of interior turnpikes and paved roads. Moving freight overland, however, remained excruciatingly slow and expensive. Soon developments in other sectors converged to encourage investment in new forms of transportation.[1]

In the 1820s, two local manufacturers, Josiah White and Erskine Hazard, imported anthracite coal from northeastern Pennsylvania and quickly realized its vast superiority over wood as a fuel. White and Hazard actively promoted anthracite and initiated efforts to build canals along the Delaware, Lehigh, and Schuylkill Rivers to bring coal down to the Quaker city. By the 1830s Pennsylvania had an extensive canal network, including the Main Line canal and cog railway that linked Philadelphia with Pittsburgh and the Ohio River. Canals were slow and cumbersome and closed during the winter, but they reduced inland freight rates as much as 90 percent.[2]

Just as the canals opened they were eclipsed by the newer technology of steam railways. By 1834 the city had rail service west to the Susquehanna River, north to Germantown and Manayunk, and east to Trenton, with connections to the New York harbor. By 1840, rail lines connected the city with Norristown, Wilmington, and Baltimore. Two years later the Philadelphia and Reading Railroad brought anthracite coal into the city from upstate. In 1854, the Pennsylvania Railroad completed its direct link to Pittsburgh, and, in 1858, to Chicago. While state money built most of the canals, Philadelphia investors, eager to remain competitive with Baltimore and New York, and with only limited state aid, rushed to build the rail lines. By 1856, the city and county had directly invested more than eight million dollars in the Pennsylvania and other railroads.[3]

The career of one of the city's leading merchants, Stephen Girard, reveals how much the profits of trade, combined with entrepreneurial leadership, contributed to Philadelphia's dynamic growth. Girard, who was born in France, became a ship captain in the West Indies while in his twenties and settled in Philadelphia in 1776. Girard was a shrewd merchant who quickly amassed a considerable fortune, at one time owning half a dozen ships. He then invested in real estate and banking and became a key figure in establishing Philadelphia as the nation's first banking center. When the First Bank of the United States dissolved in 1811, Girard bought the building and opened the Bank of Stephen Girard. During the War of 1812, Girard helped finance much of the federal debt. When he died, Girard left the city several million dollars for civic improvements, including building Delaware Avenue along the waterfront. His largest bequest endowed a boarding school for white male orphans known as Girard College, which opened in 1848 on a forty-three acre campus on the city's outskirts.

In 1800 Philadelphia was the nation's largest producer of hand-crafted goods, and through the first half of the century traditional lines of industry, such as apparel, furniture, and hardware still dominated local production. But the future lay in the emergence of entirely new technologies, notably factory-made textiles and machinery. Since the 1790s, water-powered spinning and weaving mills had grown up along the region's streams. By 1800, there were eight mills along Wissahickon Creek at the village of Roxborough. In the 1820s, completion of a short canal along the Schuylkill River provided the sites for several small mills in Manayunk, which rapidly grew into a major textile center. By 1850, more than twelve thousand people throughout the region worked in spinning and weaving mills.[4]

Most early textile manufacturers were men of obscure origins who started with rented machines and mill space. The career of Joseph Ripka, for example, illustrates the risks of entrepreneurship and the possibilities open to immigrants. Born in Germany, Ripka worked as a journeyman weaver when he settled in the city in 1816. By the 1830s, he owned mills in Manayunk, Pen-

Joseph Ripka used this 1850s print to advertise his mills along the north bank of the Schuylkill River in Manayunk. A short canal on the river provided water power that contributed to Manayunk's development as a textile village on the outskirts of the city. Some of Manayunk's early mills are now loft apartments. (W. H. Rease and the Library Company of Philadelphia.)

nypack, and the city proper. He steadily reinvested his profits, installed power looms early, and ruthlessly cut wages at every opportunity. By the 1850s, with upwards of a thousand workers, he ranked among the country's largest textile operators, but Ripka sold almost entirely to the South and was forced into bankruptcy by the Civil War. After the war, others purchased his buildings and resumed textile production.

Drawing on nearby supplies of iron and local technical and entrepreneurial talent, Philadelphia also became the nation's leading center of metalworking and steam engine construction. Oliver Evans and Mathias Baldwin were among the many entrepreneurs who created the basis for the city's dominating role in those industries. Evans, one of early America's most creative inventors, provided much of the early impetus. In the 1780s, he developed a fully automated grist mill. Moving to Philadelphia in 1792, he opened a machine shop, and in 1803 he built a high-pressure steam engine, a key development in U.S. industrialization that soon was powering steamboats and later railroads. In 1806, Evans built an extensive machine works on the edge of town at Ninth and Market Streets where he erected more than a hundred engines.[5]

In 1819, the year Evans died, Mathias Baldwin, a young journeyman, set up a jewelry shop. Restless and creative, he shifted to producing printing tools and equipment and in 1828 built a small steam engine to run his shop.

In 1832, Baldwin received a contract to build locomotives for the new Germantown and Norristown Railroad. In 1837 he relocated to a new factory on North Broad Street, where he became one of the nation's largest manufacturers of locomotives. Baldwin was also an active philanthropist and contributed to the construction of numerous churches. He was a delegate to the 1837 state constitutional convention, where he forcefully opposed stripping African Americans of their franchise.[6]

Philadelphia was also a leader in such diverse sectors as chemicals and shipbuilding. The chemicals industry, which included medicines, dyes, and paints, contributed valuable export commodities. Inexpensive anthracite coal provided a critical competitive advantage for those energy-intensive processes. Unfortunately, those industries dumped tons of caustic and toxic chemicals into the nearby creeks and rivers. Shipbuilding employed hundreds along the Delaware River waterfront in Kensington and Southwark, led by the U.S. Navy Yard at the foot of Federal Street. Shipbuilders benefited from extensive interdependence with the metal- and woodworking industries, with which they exchanged valuable technological knowledge.[7]

Philadelphia also emerged as the leading center of America medicine. Several pioneering doctors who emphasized anatomy as a fundamental teaching tool put the city at the forefront of medical education at the University of Pennsylvania and Jefferson Medical College. The county charity hospital at Blockley Almshouse in West Philadelphia (later Philadelphia General Hospital) and the Municipal Hospital for Contagious and Infectious Diseases were also invaluable resources for medical training. Confirming its preeminence in medicine, the city hosted the founding meeting of the American Medical Association in 1847. Soon after, Women's Medical College, the first school to train female physicians, and Homeopathic (later Hahnemann) Medical College of Pennsylvania Hospital opened.[8]

The entrepreneurial spirit of White, Hazard, Baldwin, Evans, and others and their willingness to invest in new industries, their continuous search for solutions to technical problems, and their confidence in their city made antebellum Philadelphia the nation's leading center of scientific expertise and manufacturing skill. To democratize and spread that knowledge, in 1824 city leaders founded the Franklin Institute to promote the "useful arts." The institute offered lectures, displays of models, and a library, but it soon focused on the promotion of new technical and scientific knowledge. Its *Journal* was the nation's leading scientific publication. Only in a large and dense city could the critical mass of talent, leadership, and capital converge to advance knowledge in that way. The founders and supporters of the Franklin Institute fertilized the seeds of industrialism and the further growth of Philadelphia.[9]

As the booming economy drew in thousands, the surging population spilled far beyond the city's original boundaries, spreading across six square miles from Columbia Street in the northern part of the city and south as far as Wharton Street, although settlement continued to hug the Delaware River. After 1798, the city prohibited new wooden structures in built-up areas, so red-brick row houses marched across the landscape, repeating the pattern of wider and taller houses facing the main streets, while cramped, narrow dwellings filled the alleys behind.

As the population spread, new municipalities appeared, the largest of which were Spring Garden, Northern Liberties, Kensington, Southwark, and Moyamensing. In addition, by 1850, five villages elsewhere in the county each had more than five thousand people: Germantown, Frankford, West Philadelphia, Manayunk, and Richmond. Although the city proper remained the largest single municipality, by 1830, the aggregate population of the adjacent territories was greater. The existing street grid was extended, but what seemed orderly in the seventeenth century was increasingly impractical in the nineteenth. The streets were narrow, the alleys behind even worse, and the lack of any diagonal streets to rapidly move traffic in and out of the center, except for Germantown, Ridge, and Passyunk Avenues, aggravated congestion and slowed commuting. The failure to set aside additional neighborhood squares ranks as the biggest missed opportunity.[10]

In an age when most people had to live near their work, and no zoning laws regulated land use, houses, stores, stables, workshops, and factories mixed together indiscriminately. The streets, unpaved or poorly maintained, teemed with a noisy bustle of carts, wagons, and wheelbarrows shuttling goods between stores, wharves, workshops, and warehouses; crates, barrels, and sacks of merchandise blocked sidewalks. Peddlers hawked food; pigs roamed the streets or wallowed in backyard sties; horses deposited gallons of urine and tons of waste on the cobblestones. The odors were pungent. In summer the dried manure, pulverized to dust by wagons and carts, suffused the air. Overworked animals sometimes died in the streets and lay where they fell until local governments collected them.[11]

Despite this jumble of activity, specialized districts began to emerge, although at midcentury, the process was still incomplete. The location of the railroad tracks had a critical effect on the city's industrial land-use patterns. In

Facing page: This 1856 map of Center City shows the railroad tracks along Pennsylvania Avenue, Market Street, Prime Street (just above Washington Street—now Washington Avenue), and South Broad Street. The numbers refer to the wards of the newly consolidated city. (J. H. Colton, New York, 1856. Author's collection.)

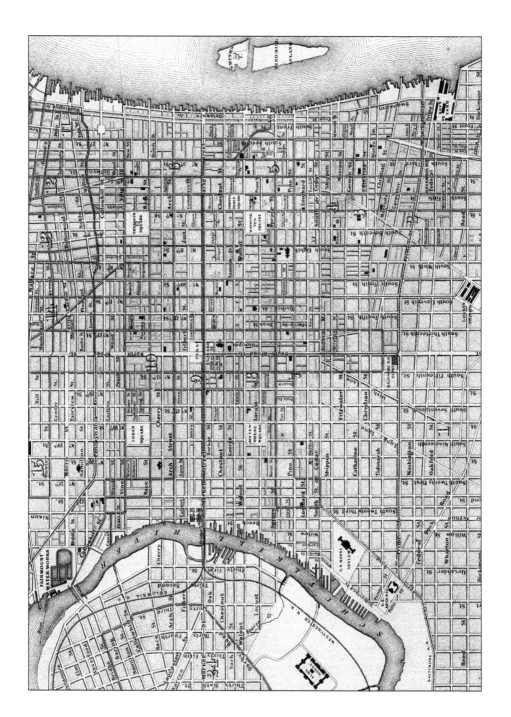

the 1830s, railroads laid tracks on both Broad and Market Streets. But the city council, fearing the noise, the speed, and the fire hazard from spewing cinders, prohibited steam locomotives within the city proper. Locomotives had to be disconnected and the cars pulled into town by horses. This policy, which remained in effect until the 1870s, had enormous consequences for the shape of modern Center City. To avoid the slow and cumbersome procedure, the railroads built their major freight depots just outside the city limits, encircling it with rail lines. The Pennsylvania Railroad entered from the west, along Lancaster Avenue, and built freight yards at Thirtieth and Market Streets. The Reading Railroad built its main terminal at Broad and Callowhill and a freight terminal at Front Street. Two rail lines ran north through Northern Liberties and Kensington. Unfortunately, because the placement of stations lacked any coordination, the stations failed to serve as anchors for neighborhoods and contributed to increasingly congested street traffic.[12]

This pattern encouraged heavy manufacturing in the surrounding districts, particularly to the north. Locomotive and related metalworking firms clustered in the Spring Garden district along rail sidings north of Vine Street and west of Broad. Steam-powered textile mills gravitated to the rail lines in Northern Liberties and Kensington. Firms requiring large amounts of space, such as shipyards, ropewalks, glass works, tanneries, brick works, and distilleries, moved to the edges of the built-up area. The rail line along Market Street and proximity to the port kept wholesaling and light manufacturing concentrated in the city proper east of Seventh Street. Here one-quarter of all the city's production workers found employment making goods that required little or no machinery or equipment, such as sails, cigars, boxes, barrels, and apparel.[13]

By the 1850s, a small business district had emerged on Third and Fourth Streets, south of Market and west along Chestnut and Walnut Streets. Three landmark buildings anchored the district: the First Bank of the United States, on Third below Chestnut (1797, later Girard Bank); the Second Bank of the United States, on Chestnut above Fourth (1824, later the U.S. Customs House), and the Merchants Exchange, at Walnut from Dock to Third (1834). In 1850, the Jayne building on Chestnut rose to an awe-inspiring eight stories. Lower Chestnut became the leading fashionable shopping street, where large glass windows and tasteful interiors attracted a growing clientele of middle-class women who promenaded along the street to see and greet one another. But retail shops were scattered widely throughout the city. A small entertainment district emerged farther north, anchored by the Chestnut Street Theater at Sixth and the Walnut Theater at Ninth (1809). In 1855, the grand Academy of Music opened at Broad and Locust near the newly emerging fashionable residential zone.[14]

This 1848 depiction of Fourth Street, just north of Market Street, shows the emerging mixed-use retail district. At the time, many buildings featured retail shops on the ground floor, with large display windows, and manufacturing above. Much commercial activity took place in the streets. The sidewalks shown here are lined with crates and casks. On the far left, a tank cart waters the street to keep the dust down; in front of number 10, a clerk or apprentice hammers a nail into a crate; at center an African American man pushes a wheelbarrow; and on the right, clerks unload wooden crates. (W. H. Rease and the Library Company of Philadelphia.)

The pace and scale of life were accelerating. People thought about time and space in a new way. For the first time, news could travel faster than men could carry it. In 1846, a telegraph line linked Philadelphia and Baltimore. The astonishing device carried business orders and commodity prices throughout the country in minutes. A rail trip to New York took only a few hours, to Pittsburgh, half a day, to Chicago, only two days. Increases in productivity brought sharp declines in the cost of manufactured goods, but most midcentury Philadelphians still labored long hours at low pay to sustain their families. The industrialization that stimulated economic growth brought in its wake new class divisions and powerful social tensions.

Peopling the Industrial City

Rapid urbanization and early industrialization fractured the social divisions of the pre-industrial world. At the extremes, the circumstances of the rich and the destitute changed little, but the eighteenth century "middle sort" fragmented into distinct middle and working classes. This change occurred gradually, and class boundaries remained permeable and fluid. People who rose in income and status might slip back in hard times.

The upper class included descendants of the same families that dominated eighteenth-century society, augmented, but not always accepted socially, by newly rich industrialists. Upper-class families resided along lower Walnut and Chestnut Streets until the 1840s, when the emerging business district pushed them west to Rittenhouse Square, where they built large townhouses and exclusive institutions, such as the elegant St. Mark's and Holy Trinity Episcopal churches, the Protestant Episcopal Academy, Penn Charter School, and the Philadelphia Club.[15]

The dynamic economy created new occupations, such as manager, agent, broker, wholesaler, bookkeeper, and clerk, that provided opportunities for many to carve out for themselves new positions in the social hierarchy as part of a white-collar middle class. Excluded from the rarefied world of the elites but eager to separate themselves from the boorish and ill-mannered, these middle-class men and women organized their own literary societies and cultural groups that hosted lectures and balls; young men also founded sports clubs. Most societies were gender segregated, but some welcomed young adults of both sexes: meeting appropriate people of the opposite sex was undoubtedly a major function. As more and more people could afford a variety of commercial entertainments, venues appeared catering to the different tastes. The cheap seats at the Academy of Music cost no more than those for the minstrel show at Sanford's Theater on Eleventh Street, but the entertainment provided and the behavior expected made it likely that the two venues attracted very distinct audiences.[16]

Although the middle classes strove to distinguish themselves socially from manual workers, their ability to do so spatially was limited. Mass transit began in 1833 with the introduction of the omnibus, a modified stagecoach in which people sat facing each other on narrow benches in a stuffy wagon as it slowly rumbled along cobblestone streets. The omnibuses served the major streets, particularly those heading west toward Rittenhouse Square. At their peak in 1858, more than two hundred omnibuses were in service, but horse-drawn streetcars on rails soon appeared that could pull larger cars at faster speeds, opening up more land area for development within a reasonable commuting time. By 1860, eighteen different lines carried thousands of passengers. In addition, from the late 1840s steam railroads offered commuter service to Germantown and Chestnut Hill. Mass transit permitted some affluent white-collar workers, such as bankers, lawyers, and merchants, to occupy large houses and spacious lots at the urban fringe. But for most middle-class and well-paid artisan families, builders offered modest two- and three-story red-

At midcentury, middle- and upper-class families could afford an expensively furnished parlor and sometimes a library. This 1861 photograph shows the family of Ferdinand J. Dreer, a wealthy businessman, relaxing in the family library. The two women are engaged in needlework. Notice the elaborate gas chandelier, marble fireplace, and framed pictures on the walls. (John Moran and the Library Company of Philadelphia.)

brick row houses that enabled Philadelphians to enjoy higher rates of home-ownership than those in other large cities.[17]

In contrast, the circumstances of Philadelphia's manual workers improved only moderately for some, and for many they grew worse. As master craftsmen and merchants sought ways to meet the increased demand for manufactured goods, they tightened supervision of journeymen and extended working hours. Masters divided work into simpler repetitive tasks so they could hire people with less training, saving only the most skilled assembly work for the artisans. Many journeymen experienced a painful and permanent loss of status and income; for others, opportunities arose in wholly new trades that employed hundreds of men as machinists, boilermakers, and gas- and steam-fitters, as well as

This 1867 photograph shows the three-story, three-room workers' cottages known as bandbox—or father, son, and holy ghost—houses on Queen Street near Front Street in Southwark. (John Moran and the Library Company of Philadelphia.)

locomotive engineers, firemen, trainmen, and conductors. In that flux, a new wage-earning working class emerged with a clear hierarchy of occupations: skilled artisans, semiskilled machine tenders, and unskilled laborers. This structure was vastly different from the master-journeyman-apprentice system of the eighteenth century with its expectation that one would move from one rank to the next.[18]

In the new hierarchy, working conditions varied widely. Everywhere people toiled in dark and dangerous workshops and factories, unheated in winter and stifling in summer. When accidents occurred, employers accepted no responsibility. Only skilled workers earned enough to support a family on a minimal budget. Women constituted a significant share of the workforce, since wives and children often had to supplement family income. Single women barely survived. Many women worked as maids; most others were employed in textile mills and garment shops. Families often sent boys out to sell newspapers, polish shoes, and scavenge for coal or firewood; girls peddled food and such items as ribbons, needles, and thread.

Some of the most oppressive working conditions could be found in the new cotton mills. The stale air was thick with cotton lint, and uncovered gears and

drive belts occasionally caught fingers, hands, and long hair with horrible results. Further, mill owners enforced rigid rules with stiff fines. Women hesitated to quit not only because they had limited options but also because
owners usually withheld two weeks' wages. The male overseers sometimes beat
children, cursed adults, and demanded sexual favors from the women. For all
that, the pay was abysmally low; two or more family members, including children, had to work for the family to survive. Elsewhere, conditions depended
heavily on skill level and industry. In small workshops close supervision and
piece rates forced workers to maintain a hectic pace. Only the most skilled
artisans were still able to set their own pace and earn a respectable income.[19]

Living conditions varied with the skill level. Artisans might enjoy a row
house with a carpet in the parlor, a cast-iron stove, an indoor water spigot, and
a flush toilet, but most workers were less fortunate. The lowest-paid unskilled
workers, often Irish immigrants and African Americans, crowded into attics,
cellars, shanties, and sheds with only public hydrants and backyard, often
filthy, privies that spilled their contents into walkways.[20]

Working-class neighborhoods emerged along the city's fringes within
walking distance of factories and workshops, in Southwark, Moyamensing,
Northern Liberties, Kensington, Richmond, and Manayunk. In those areas,
workers were able to create a cultural life independent of middle- and upper-class supervision or control. They gathered in the streets, in saloons, clubs,
and associations, and in meetings of the struggling trade union movement. For
men, associational life often centered on neighborhood and ethnic-based volunteer fire companies. Fire companies functioned much like working-class
fraternities, and by the 1850s there were more than seventy, most with their
own fire houses built with members' dues and neighborhood contributions.
Even less disciplined were the street gangs, many of which lasted for decades,
with such colorful names as Rats, Flayers, Smashers, Tormentors, Moyamensing Killers, and Schuylkill Rangers. Although the nineteenth-century journalist George Foster, a keen observer of urban life, depicted most gang members
as boys in their teens eager for a good time but rarely dangerous, some dealt in
theft, prostitution, and extortion. As with the fire companies, local politicians
also found them useful at elections.[21]

Fire companies, saloons, and gangs, along with parades and religious re-
vivals, provided working people social and emotional outlets, but none addressed the rapid changes squeezing their incomes and eroding their status. In
the 1820s and 1830s Philadelphia saw the country's first workers' political
party and a labor movement sufficiently well organized to briefly sustain a
general strike. The Working Men's Party, made up of skilled artisans, not
factory operatives, survived only a few years, but in 1834 seventeen separate

craft groups formed an umbrella organization, the General Trades' Union, which soon had fifty affiliates representing almost ten thousand workers. In May 1835, Irish coal heavers, among the lowest-paid workers, struck for shorter hours, and the strike quickly spread as other trades joined. Upwards of twenty thousand workers participated in a strike for a ten-hour day that proved successful in many trades; by the 1850s the ten-hour day was standard in most workplaces. The strike in 1835 was the first such general strike in the nation's history and provided the greatest display of worker solidarity in the city before 1910. In 1837, however, a severe business depression wiped out the General Trades' Union, and by the 1840s unionism was again moribund. In their frustration, many workers lashed out at African Americans and immigrants.[22]

Philadelphia's modest African American community was nevertheless the largest of any northern city and engendered jealousy and resentment well beyond its actual numbers. Over the decades residential segregation increased, with the largest cluster of blacks in the side alleys and narrow courts from Lombard to Bainbridge between Fifth and Eighth Streets. Aside from a small number of sympathetic Quakers and abolitionists, Philadelphia was a profoundly racist city; most northern whites had difficulty adjusting to the presence of a free black population. Irish immigrants in particular feared that competition from black workers would undercut their already meager wages. Between 1829 and 1849 the black community suffered five major race riots, during which marauding gangs broke into black homes and smashed furniture, beating and sometimes murdering residents. Philadelphia city authorities made an effort to protect black lives and property, but those in adjacent Southwark and Moyamensing did little and often blamed blacks for instigating the disturbances. Compounding these indignities, in 1838, when Pennsylvania ratified a new constitution that eliminated the property qualification for voting, it completely disenfranchised African Americans. Thus, even those few who had met the property qualification lost their vote.[23]

Discrimination and prejudice kept most blacks in abject poverty. The only jobs open to them were physically demanding, demeaning, low paying, and insecure: 80 percent of men held unskilled jobs, mostly as laborers or servants. A lucky few held more secure positions as porters, barbers, drivers, messengers, stevedores, and, in a business blacks had developed, caterers. Even those with artisan skills frequently could not practice them. More than 80 percent of employed women toiled as domestics or laundresses. Another 14 percent were seamstresses, the lowest paying of all skilled trades. Further, after 1840, Irish immigrants increasingly pushed blacks out of the few occupations they had dominated. By 1850, the share of African Americans among construction laborers and stevedores, for example, had fallen to a mere 1 percent. Discrimination kept blacks entirely out of the new mills and factories and from almost any job that offered opportunity to learn skills. A handful of doctors, teachers, ministers, and peddlers comprised a small middle class.[24]

In the face of such hardships African Americans sustained their own institutions and developed their own leaders. Their churches and fraternal lodges provided mutual assistance, material and emotional, and nurtured leadership skills. Away from the watchful and patronizing gaze of whites, they could assert their personal worth. By 1847 Philadelphia had 106 all-black beneficial societies, essentially insurance groups providing small sickness and death benefits.[25] African Americans relied on their clergy and a few successful businessmen, such as James Forten and Robert Purvis, for leadership. Forten was born free in the city to a sailmaker and benefited from some formal education. He was able to establish himself as a sailmaker and his business prospered. Over many decades Forten was a vigorous and outspoken advocate for black rights and an end to slavery. He gave William Lloyd Garrison of Boston money to start the abolitionist newspaper *The Liberator* and served as vice president of the American Anti-Slavery Society. To assist runaways and protect black citizens from being kidnapped into slavery, in 1837 black Philadelphians founded the Vigilant Association, which hid and fed fugitives and spirited them quickly out of the city. James Forten's son-in-law, Robert Purvis, the son of a free black woman and a British merchant, played a leading role in the association.[26]

Philadelphia's dynamic economy also attracted large numbers of European immigrants in search of new opportunities. Immigration surged in the ten years after 1845 as thousands of destitute Irish fled the potato famine. German immigrants, dislocated by industrialism and political upheavals at home, soon joined them. By 1860, 170,000 immigrants constituted 30 percent of the total population and an even larger share of the adult population; two-thirds came from Ireland. The famine Irish had few skills or assets and no experience with urban living. They entered the workforce at the bottom and struggled for decades to advance, performing most of the city's common labor. Irish women often worked as domestics or as unskilled operatives in the textile mills. The German migration was quite distinct from the Irish. Many German immigrants arrived with craft skills and had less difficulty finding work. They also more quickly established social institutions. German immigration augmented the minute Jewish community. In the 1840s there were fewer than two thousand Jews; by 1860, there were eight thousand. There was also a steady stream of English and Scottish immigrants, mostly to the textile trades. Prejudice favored the British and German immigrants, who found work that offered opportunities to learn skills and advance.[27]

Since the city lacked a large supply of old and inexpensive housing in the central district, no real immigrant ghetto emerged before the Civil War. Irish and German immigrants could be found everywhere. But there were distinct clusters that revealed the differences between the two groups and how the city was changing. Germans were overrepresented in the emerging factory districts in the northeast corner of the city proper, as well as in Northern Liberties and Kensington. There was also a smaller cluster in Southwark, mostly of German Jews in the needle trades. The Irish were more spread out than the Germans but were overrepresented in areas of cheap housing and access to unskilled work: Southwark, Moyamensing, Gray's Ferry, and Richmond. British immigrants clustered near the textile mills, in Kensington, Manayunk, Germantown, and Frankford.[28]

A large segment of the community resented the new immigrants. Native-born workers already felt under siege from the rapid changes and feared increased competition from new arrivals crowding the job market and depressing wages. English and German immigrants, particularly those with skills, met with little resistance, but major clashes occurred between Irish Catholic immigrants and the Anglo-Protestant majority. The antipathy between Protestants and Catholics stretched back hundreds of years. Protestants, fearing all Catholics would take orders from their clergy, believed that Catholicism was antithetical to democratic institutions.[29]

The anti-immigrant nativists coalesced around the issue of Bible reading in the public schools. For ambitious families of all classes the public schools were a key institution for their children's social advancement. The state had mandated that schools use the Protestant King James Bible to teach reading, but Catholics viewed this rule as an attack on their rights to freedom of religion and access to a free public education. The Catholic bishop sought to remove all Bible reading from the schools, which nativists viewed as a direct attack on Protestantism and indirectly on all American values that they self-righteously believed stemmed from Protestant Christianity. As far as most Protestants were concerned, use of the King James Bible represented a nonsectarian education; furthermore, from the nativists' viewpoint, it was the Catholic children who most needed the Bible reading. The controversy reinforced the nativists' worst fears and prejudices.[30]

In 1844, the escalating tensions exploded in two cataclysmic riots. In May, a provocative nativist rally in the heart of an Irish Catholic Kensington neighborhood led to a week of rioting during which mobs destroyed several homes and burned a convent and two Irish Catholic churches. After at least six fatalities the state militia finally restored order, but it proved to be merely a lull in the action. In July another riot broke out in Southwark around the

This composite sketch of the Anti-Catholic Riots of 1844 suggests the mayhem that occurred. But note that the artist took considerable liberties, since the rioters most likely did not wear high hats and dress coats. (*Free Library of Philadelphia*, Print and Picture Collection.)

St. Philip de Neri Catholic Church, which the state militia was defending. Two men were killed when a mob tried to storm the church and General George Cadwalader ordered the militia to fire. The mob responded by rolling a cannon from the waterfront onto Christian Street, discharging a volley at the militia and killing two more. In the ensuing battle both sides fired cannons down the narrow, crowded streets. At least twelve more men were killed, two of them militiamen, and at least forty-three were wounded. The Southwark riot, which required two thousand troops to restore order, gave Philadelphia a reputation as an anti-Catholic city.[31]

Urban Politics in Peace and War

No one in 1800 could have conceived of or planned for the surging population growth of the subsequent half century. Recurrent epidemics, periodic riots, chronic rowdyism, a flood of immigrants, and industrialization cried out for new institutions to maintain civic peace, protect public health, and address social inequities, but there was no model to follow. Philadelphians had to grope their way toward an unknown future and experiment with different solutions. The first sixty years of the century was a period of extraordinary institution building. Visionary leaders stepped forward to implement solutions to some of the city's most urgent problems. In other areas, however, the social needs of the majority received less attention.

With racial and nativist tensions forming a backdrop, Philadelphia's middle and upper classes felt besieged. They certainly embraced the wealth that industrial capitalism created and tolerated the workers necessary to produce it, yet they feared increased taxation and the rising rates of crime and poverty. Rather than consider low pay, especially for women, and recurrent unemployment as the root causes of poverty, they found it easier to blame moral or character flaws, or even charity itself, which, in the view of many, only encouraged idleness and begging. As in the eighteenth century, opinion makers often labeled the indigent "idle and vicious." Such views became convenient excuses for punitive policies that reduced aid when it was needed most. Large numbers lived on the edge of want, but the demeaning conditions surrounding charity, by design, sufficiently deterred all but the most desperate. Between 1800 and 1850 the share of the population receiving public relief rose, while annual public spending per recipient fell from $34 to about $5.20.[32]

The preferred solution was to modify behavior through exhortation, regulation, and sometimes incarceration. Because many believed incarceration, with a strict regimen of order and discipline, would change behavior, it was a great age for the founding of prisons, almshouses, orphanages, and insane asylums. The most extreme case was the Eastern State Penitentiary, where the hapless inmates were kept in solitary confinement to reflect on their sins until many of them went insane. Philadelphia also maintained its strong tradition of private charity, with women often taking the lead. Quakers and evangelical Protestants dominated the largest charity, the Union Benevolent Association, which organized two hundred middle-class, white women who visited the poor, offering a strong dose of moralism with small amounts of aid. The association was suspicious of "indiscriminate giving," but, unlike many other charities, it included blacks and did not excessively proselytize to Catholics; in 1851, it was helping twenty-one hundred families, including offering free baths, a dispensary, and short-term lodgings.[33]

Despite the existence of these voluntary associations, decentralized authority remained the hallmark of municipal governance. In Philadelphia proper, the city council established separate agencies to deal with specific functions—such as provision of water and gas—that reported directly to the council. Although patronage was limited, it remained firmly in the hands of the councilmen. Each ward elected its own assessors, tax collectors, magistrate, and, later, school directors. Participatory democracy meant politicians had to appeal to a broad constituency. While private enterprise was creating large institutions to manage complex economic functions, such as banks and railroads, in governance a lingering fear of centralized authority kept power fragmented. Business and community leaders, however, including Stephen Girard, Mathias Baldwin, and James Forten, demonstrated remarkable vision and foresight in broadening the notion of civic responsibility. In these years Philadelphia achieved its two greatest civic accomplishments of the nineteenth century: a publicly owned water works and a large urban park.

The yellow fever epidemics of the 1790s highlighted the inadequacy of the ad hoc and volunteer arrangements by which eighteenth century citizens managed their affairs. A belief that dirty streets and contaminated drinking water spread the disease led the city council to explore ways to build a water system to protect public health and to fight fires. In 1799, Benjamin Henry Latrobe, a young British engineer living in the city, proposed a novel scheme to use steam-powered pumps to lift water from the Schuylkill River to tanks at Center Square and distribute it through wooden pipes. Steam power was a new technology, and there were only a few steam engines in the country, but with the leadership of merchants and city councilmen Henry Drinker Jr. and Thomas Pym Cope, the council took a chance on the ambitious scheme. In 1801, the Philadelphia Water Works began operation. It was the first public water system in a large U.S. city. Individual homes could connect to the system for five dollars a year or obtain water free from public hydrants. Although polluted drinking water did not spread yellow fever, after 1800 such epidemics were fewer and less deadly. Public water meant that people did not need to keep backyard rain barrels, and that the streets could be periodically flushed, in both cases reducing the number of stagnant pools of water where mosquitoes bred.

Before long the steam engines running the water works proved woefully inefficient, and in 1822 a new system was completed that used water-powered pumps to lift water to a reservoir at Fairmount Hill (site of the current Philadelphia Museum of Art). The rebuilt system had ample capacity and was extended to serve the adjacent municipalities. The elaborate, classical buildings of the engine house at Centre Square and later the pumping works along the Schuylkill River reflected the enormous pride the city took in this great civic achievement. The water works reaffirmed the supremacy of the public interest and mutual responsibility of all citizens in a democratic society. Vindication for the water works came in 1832, when a virulent cholera epidemic swept across the nation and the death rate in Philadelphia was only a quarter that of New York, which lacked any good supply of clean water.[34]

Philadelphia's second great municipal achievement, the creation of Fairmount Park, also came out of efforts to protect the quality of city water. In 1828, the city council purchased twenty-four acres upstream of the water intake, and the state prohibited dumping any "noxious or offensive matter" into the river. The five-acre landscaped grounds immediately surrounding the pumping station became a popular attraction, visited by such dignitaries as General Lafayette and Charles Dickens. At the urging of Cope in the 1840s, the city council also purchased the country estate of Lemon Hill, even though it was outside the city limits at the time. For a decade, Lemon Hill was leased out as a beer garden, but in 1855 the city dedicated Lemon Hill as a public park amid growing national interest in landscaped parks as antidotes to "unnatural" urban life. Meanwhile, Cope and other civic leaders solicited funds to acquire an adjacent thirty-three-acre estate, which the city bought in 1858 and merged with Lemon Hill to create Fairmount Park. Unlike New York's Central Park, which was built at the same time, Fairmount Park already possessed considerable natural beauty, in no small part because it overlooked the river. An imaginative plan to landscape the original 110 acres, although delayed by the Civil War, was eventually carried out.[35]

The tradition of civic leadership was also manifest in the establishment of a host of institutions dedicated to the accumulation and dissemination of knowledge and to nurturing cultural expression. Beginning in 1818 countywide schools offered classes for poor white children but relied on older children supervising the younger ones. Learning consisted mostly of rote memorization and discipline was harsh, but the schools were cheap. In 1837, a thoroughly reorganized system offered a free, though noncompulsory, education for all children. Still, taxpayers remained stingy in their support; in 1843, there were sixty-six students for each teacher and the classrooms were often dismal. Poor children were unlikely to attend; in 1867, twenty thousand children ages six to eighteen were neither in school nor working. In 1838 the city council established Central High School for boys, the first such public academy in the country, and, a decade later, Girls Normal School (later the High School for Girls). Night schools offered vocational courses, but investment in education failed to keep up with the city's growth.[36]

Outside of the public arena, private organizations primarily served an upper- and middle-class audience, but they contributed greatly to the cultural and educational life of the city. The Academy of Fine Arts, the Academy of Natural Sciences, and the Historical Society of Pennsylvania educated and enriched people's lives. The American Philosophical Society remained the nation's leading scientific institution. Two new subscription libraries, the Athenaeum and the Mercantile Library, provided greater access to books and ideas. Charles Wilson Peale's museum in Independence Hall exposed the public to fine art and natural history. The Academy of Music provided a venue for concerts. Social elites founded and dominated those organizations, which helped cement Philadelphia's place among the nation's leading cultural and intellectual centers.[37]

An interlocking network of families, many the descendants of colonial elites, controlled the major business and civic institutions and, at least until the 1840s, filled important positions in the government of the city proper. For example, Joseph Ingersoll, leader of one of the city's oldest families, was president of the Academy of Fine Arts and sat on the boards of the Bank of the United States, the University of Pennsylvania, the Historical Society, and the House of Refuge. While this concentration of power meant that the interests of the elites were protected, it also meant that leaders maintained a civic vision. But those families were notoriously slow to admit newly wealthy businessmen to their ranks. Their snobbery imparted a conservative ethos to the city.[38]

By midcentury, however, the vision that characterized the civic leadership was fading. Rather than focusing on community welfare, politicians and businessmen now showed more concern about taxes. At the same time, however, Philadelphia's extraordinary growth and demand for water exceeded the system's capacity, requiring new capital investments to protect the quality and the supply of water. Although the adjacent municipalities built their own water works, with little regional coordination or planning, the city was experiencing a growing shortage of clean water. The Kensington Water Works, opened in 1850, drew its supply from the increasingly contaminated Delaware River. Lack of adequate potable water took its toll. More than a thousand people died in the cholera epidemic of 1849, mostly in the overcrowded sections of Southwark and Moyamensing, prompting doctors to advocate mandatory connections of all new homes to water mains. But local officials rejected the proposal as an imposition on private property rights. The pride of the city in the first half of the century would become a notorious scandal by the end. In addition, congested housing, filthy streets, communal privies in overcrowded alleys and courts, and the almost complete absence of bathing facilities took a heavy toll on public health. The cost of improvements would fall on property owners and landlords, while the cost of neglect, in higher rates of sickness and death, fell on the working classes.[39]

By the 1840s, concern mounted over the recurrent rioting and brawling. Immediately after the 1844 riot came calls for a unified police department and even for consolidation of the entire county into one government to stem the mounting violence. The lack of any effective police department and the fragmentation of the county between the city and twenty-eight surrounding districts allowed the violence of 1844 to get out of hand. A mob need only dash across a district boundary to avoid a local constable. The rowdyism, especially by gangs and fire companies, continued to worsen, with at least eighty-three serious violent episodes during the decade involving twenty-six different gangs. After the 1849 race riot, the state established a united police department with an elected police marshal.

Local politicians in the city proper, which supported the Whig Party, and surrounding municipalities, which supported the Democrats, resisted consolidation, fearing loss of power and autonomy. But the suburban districts recognized the need for the urban services a consolidated city could deliver. In 1853, in the name of efficiency and order, a coalition of business leaders and supporters of the nativist Prohibition Party, hoping to control immigrants by restricting alcohol, managed to get a pro-consolidation slate elected to the Pennsylvania Assembly. The consolidation advocates established the blue-ribbon Committee of One Hundred to draft a charter. In 1854, the state legislature unified the city and county of Philadelphia; there was no countywide referendum on the question.[40]

To build support among the outlying districts and townships, the charter placed heavy emphasis on local democracy. Although the new ward boundaries were drawn to weaken existing loyalties and ethnic rivalries, the charter fragmented power when greater centralization was sorely needed. Each ward would elect representatives to a two-chamber city council, as well as electing tax assessors, school directors, and guardians of the poor. The new council started with a cumbersome ninety-eight members, and, as the city grew, rather than redrawing ward boundaries, it created new wards, steadily enlarging the number of members and laying the foundation for powerful ward-based professional politicians to control nominations, manipulate elections, and allocate patronage. The council also used its power over expenditures to meddle in the administrative functions of the thirty-plus separate departments and agencies. Adding further confusion, the charter preserved separate county government offices, with some overlapping jurisdictions between city and county officials.

The consolidated City of Philadelphia held 565,000 people in 130 square miles. It was a truly regional city, in area the largest city in the country; its boundaries have not changed since. The new city moved quickly to streamline and modernize city functions and create a centralized bureaucracy. The new government expanded Fairmount Park, installed a police and fire telegraph system, put the police in uniforms, and gained greater control over the fire companies (leading to the establishment of a professional fire department in 1871), measures that cut down on some of the rowdiness and rioting. Streets were renamed to eliminate duplication, and house numbering was rationalized across the city. Despite the cumbersome charter, consolidation provided an opportunity to shape the future growth and character of the nation's second largest city. The city took control of the water and gas networks and extended both. Whether the citizens and leaders could rise to the challenge remained to be seen.[41]

Politics in the new city, however, provided little room for cooperation. The first mayor, a nativist, refused to appoint any immigrants to the new police force and tried to enforce laws banning Sunday alcohol sales, but neither policy went over well with the rapidly growing immigrant community. The second mayor, Richard Vaux, a Democrat, brought immigrants into the police force but was defeated in his bid for reelection in a city that tended to support the Whig Party and their platform of protective tariffs and activist program of economic development. With the city's close economic ties to the South, and hostility toward its relatively large black population, both parties opposed abolition as dangerous to the union.

Because Quakers had taken the lead in opposition to slavery, Philadelphia emerged as a center of the abolition movement. The American Anti-Slavery Society held its founding meeting in Philadelphia in 1833. Its supporters considered slavery immoral and called for its immediate abolition with no compensation for slaveholders. Most whites found that position a dangerous threat to the Union and particularly to the city with its ties to the South. Some abolitionists stirred up additional animosity by advocating equal rights for women. Since many venues, fearing violence, refused to rent meeting space to abolitionists, in May 1838 they put up their own building, Pennsylvania Hall, on Sixth Street near Race. With access to an auditorium seating three thousand, several antislavery groups planned events during the first week. Inside, in keeping with their beliefs of equality, men and women of both races sat together. This practice was offensive to most whites because the mixing of genders and races raised profound fears of miscegenation, which they called "amalgamation." As rumors of amalgamation and of dangerous abolitionist doctrines swept through the city, mobs surrounded the building every evening, intent on disrupting the proceedings. More than once the mayor tried to persuade them to disperse. On the third night a mob set the building on fire. A crowd of perhaps fifteen thousand gathered to cheer as it burned to the ground, refusing to let firemen attack the flames. In the long run, the destruction of Pennsylvania Hall brought new recruits to abolitionism because people feared the implication of slavery for free speech.[42]

Twenty-two years later, Abraham Lincoln narrowly won Philadelphia in the 1860 election, but he ran on a ticket labeled the People's Party whose platform emphasized a high tariff and downplayed the slavery issue. With the outbreak of the Civil War in April 1861, the city rallied to the Union cause, and Philadelphia's vast industrial sector shifted heavily to war production. Three federal facilities played key roles. The Quartermaster's Schuylkill Arsenal kept five thousand women busy sewing uniforms in their homes, while the Frankford Arsenal, with twelve hundred men, produced most of the small arms for the Union. Another three thousand worked at the Navy Yard building eleven major warships. Thousands of others worked at shipyards, foundries, machine and metal shops, textile mills, and garment shops throughout the city on war materiel. The army constructed the country's two largest military hospitals in the city, confirming its dominance as the nation's leading medical center. The war did not accelerate industrialization, but it put handsome profits into the coffers of some local manufacturers.

The war had a mixed effect on everyday life. The city grew more crowded as war production attracted migrants and immigrants while residential construction slowed. As inflation pushed up prices, workers turned again to trade unions, which grew stronger with shortages of skilled workers. Because of the military and industrial manpower demands, even the almshouse population fell. The city council authorized $1.50 a week to aid the families of soldiers, triple the amount the guardians of the poor provided for relief. In June 1863, leading African Americans, with white allies, raised several "colored regiments," which fought in several battles late in the war. Mayor Alexander Henry and a professional police department worked effectively to maintain order at key moments. As a result, Philadelphia experienced little unrest during the war, avoiding the notorious draft and race riots that erupted in New York.[43]

Despite a faction of Democrats who sought reconciliation with the South, Republicans strengthened their hold on the city, particularly after the Union victory at Gettysburg on July 1–3, led by Philadelphia's own General George Meade. Although by 1864 the Democrats embraced a pro-war position, by then they were fatally tainted as unpatriotic. The Republicans further solidified their support with a high protective tariff popular with both workers and employers. The sharp increases in the tariff had a bigger long-term effect on Philadelphia, as the center of American machine production, than did the war itself. Running on the Union Party label, Lincoln carried the city in 1864, and his party swept the city council. Those victories laid the basis for Republican dominance in Philadelphia politics that lasted almost ninety years, perhaps the most enduring effect of the war in the city.

———————

AS IN THE PREVIOUS CENTURY, men of prominence and vision stepped forward to identify and address pressing needs. In building the water works, creating Fairmount Park, and consolidating the entire urban region, Philadelphia led the nation. For all citizens, a prosperous city that offered ample employment was probably the highest priority, yet the harsh working and living conditions received scant attention.

3

INDUSTRY TRIUMPHANT/
CIVIC FAILURE

1865–1930

I N 1876 THE UNITED STATES CELEBRATED its centennial year with a great world's fair in Philadelphia's Fairmount Park. Ten million people came from across the country and around the world to see the fair and America's second largest city. Philadelphians had taken the lead in organizing the fair and its success was a source of enormous pride. Visitors saw a city that was among the world's great manufacturing centers. Its economy shaped the city's structure and attracted a staggering population, far exceeding anything that had come before. From 1860 to 1930 Philadelphia's population jumped from 566,000 to 1.9 million and filled out much of its open space. Center City expanded into a modern and diversified downtown with skyscrapers and landmark civic buildings. Although the economic prosperity raised people's material standard of living, compared with other large cities, Philadelphia failed to live up to its potential. In this era prosperity eclipsed the public welfare. With responsible leadership, conditions could have been far better.

Private City/Public City

In the decades after the war, Philadelphia nurtured an extraordinarily productive and profitable economy. By the early twentieth century, the manufacturing sector produced almost $750 million of goods, employing 250,000 wage and 41,000 salaried workers. The city was home to such nationally famous consumer brands as Stetson hats, Fels-Naptha soap, Whitman's chocolates, Burpee seeds, and the *Saturday Evening Post* and the *Ladies' Home*

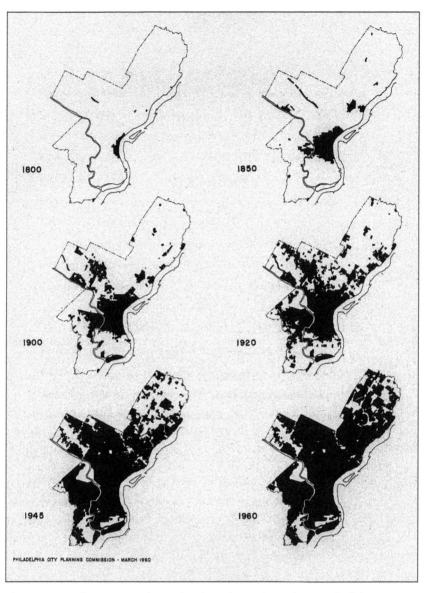

This sequence of maps, using the modern boundaries, shows the growth of the city from 1800 to 1960. Until 1900 the population remained compact. After 1900 the electric trolley and subway/elevated rapid transit enabled the population to spread farther out. But even in 1945 the city's fringe boasted considerable open space, especially in the Northeast. (City Planning Commission, *Comprehensive Plan: The Physical Development Plan for the City of Philadelphia* [Philadelphia, 1960]. Special Collections Research Center, Temple University Libraries, Philadelphia, PA.)

Many women worked in manufacturing, mostly in textile and garment shops. In this photograph taken around 1910, women trim hats at the mammoth Stetson factory at Fourth and Montgomery Streets in Kensington. Notice the large, well-lit room, an improvement over the dark and crowded conditions of many sweatshops and mills. John B. Stetson, a leader in what was known as "welfare capitalism," offered his workers amenities and benefits. (Library Company of Philadelphia.)

Journal. Three attributes accounted for the strength of the manufacturing base: its diversity, its flexibility, and its decentralized structure. The diversity meant firms and workers possessed an astonishing array of technical skills that often could be transferred from one product to another; it also meant that the economy could absorb cyclical slowdowns in one sector. The flexibility permitted the manufacture of specialized or customized products, produced in small batches, which made it easy to shift production to meet new styles. The decentralized structure meant thousands of small businesses, with an ability and willingness to adapt products and processes, anchored the manufacturing sector. Those attributes led to a manufacturing style that was profitable for firms and provided a large number of skilled jobs for workers.[1]

The strength of this system can be demonstrated in two great industrial complexes: textiles and garments, and metalworking and heavy machinery. Textile production remained Philadelphia's largest industry by far. Early in the new century, textiles employed sixty-five thousand people in the region, accounting for 10 percent of the nation's textile workforce and almost a quarter of the city's wage earners. But firms remained small, with an industry average of eighty-three workers specializing in one phase of production, such as spinning, weaving, knitting, dyeing, or finishing. Independent pattern designers worked closely with proprietors to introduce new styles. Thus, the entire industry was highly interdependent and firms relied heavily on the pool of experienced skilled workers, male and female, to meet the demand. Kensington held the largest concentration of textile factories and workers; with more than a hundred thousand people living cheek by jowl in narrow row houses, it was essentially a dense mill town in the midst of a large city.

The large garment industry, clustered in Center City and adjacent Southwark, complemented textiles. German Jewish owners dominated the business, with most of the work done by more recently arrived Russian Jews and Italians. Here too, a decentralized structure made firms interdependent as people carried goods back and forth between shops and homes, keeping Southwark one of the most overcrowded sections of the city. Competition was fierce and wages low.[2]

Philadelphia was also the center of an interdependent network of machine tool builders, specialty foundries, and machine shops. In 1900, Philadelphia's workforce included thirty-one thousand machinists and metal trades workers. Baldwin Locomotives and William Cramp and Sons, shipbuilders, anchored the industry. For more than half a century, the Baldwin Locomotive Works, the world's largest steam locomotive manufacturer, annually accounted for between 30 and 45 percent of total U.S. output. To roll out a customized locomotive in as few as eight weeks required a large force of skilled designers, draftsmen, tool and die makers, iron molders, blacksmiths, and machinists. By 1900, the Baldwin Locomotive Works sprawled across eight square blocks north and west from Broad and Callowhill, and in 1906, its peak year, more than seventeen thousand workers produced an average of 8.5 engines a day. In addition, the company subcontracted half of its parts, sustaining metalworking shops throughout the district. This interconnected network of firms and men with complementary skills enabled large and small businesses to work together to solve technological problems and contributed to the fourfold increase in the productivity of Baldwin workers.[3]

Philadelphia was also a preeminent center of shipbuilding and machine tools. The city's early lead and strong dominance in the manufacture of stationary steam engines, and the depth of skills among its workers, enabled the city's leading yards to make the transition from wood to steam. Cramp's shipyards in Kensington, which built many of the navy's new iron and steel ships, including the battleship *Maine,* ranked as the nation's largest shipbuilder. Among the most complex of all capital goods, each ship was a custom product. In the mid-1890s the company directly employed about five thousand workers, but several times that number worked for suppliers and contractors that

Hundreds of small, specialty metal shops made parts and components for the city's manufacturers. Typical was the Eagle Builders Iron Works on St. John (now American) Street in Kensington, shown in this photograph taken around 1899. The machinery was powered by a basement steam engine linked to the power shaft that ran along the ceiling of the shop. Leather belts connected the individual machines lined up along the wall to the power shafts. (Library Company of Philadelphia [unidentified photographer].)

were involved in producing a single ship. For example, William Sellers and Company, the nation's preeminent machine tool builders, supplied much of the heavy equipment for firms such as Baldwin and Cramp at its Bush Hill works and at Midvale Steel in Nicetown. At both plants William and his cousin, Coleman, promoted research on tool steels and ways to improve productivity. At Midvale some of this work was turned over to Frederick Winslow Taylor, whose time and motion studies pioneered the field of industrial engineering.[4]

A. Shoenhut and Company exemplified the thousands of specialty firms that dominated niche markets. Albert Shoenhut, son and grandson of toy makers, emigrated from Germany in 1866 and soon began manufacturing toy pianos in a converted storefront, eventually producing thirteen different models, one with thirty-seven keys. In 1883 seventeen men and boys worked in his small factory. By 1900, with 125 workers, he had built his own factory in Frankford and expanded into novelty toys. Shoenhut's sixty different "Rolly Dollys" had rounded, weighted bottoms that rolled upright when pushed over. In the 1920s, with more than four hundred workers, Shoenhut and Company produced the enormously popular Humpty Dumpty Circus—wooden and papier-mâché circus animals and performers with moveable joints.[5]

In an era before planning and zoning, factories were widely dispersed throughout the city. Nevertheless, specialized patterns of land use emerged. The sorting out of functions that began early in the nineteenth century was fully delineated by the end of the century, leaving a well-defined central business district; areas of deteriorated housing nearby, occupied mostly by recent immigrants and African Americans; industrial districts of factories, mills, and workshops mixed with the working-class population, mostly to the north of Center City; and, farther out, middle-class residential sections made accessible by mass transit.

The key factors shaping the city were the terrain itself, the railroads, mass transit, and Fairmount Park. The lack of natural barriers to expansion, notably in comparison with Boston and New York, enabled Philadelphia to spread easily to the north, south, and west. Four new bridges built across the Schuylkill River right after the Civil War accelerated development to the west, and a grid of streetcar routes converged on an emerging business district. In the 1890s, the streetcar lines consolidated into one company and switched to the more efficient electric trolley, making possible a uniform five-cent fare with free transfers and faster service that led to a surge in ridership. After the Civil War, banks and financial firms concentrated on Chestnut and Walnut between Fourth and Sixth Streets. Law firms clustered opposite Independence Hall, which housed city offices and the courthouse. Stock brokers, importers, and insurance firms dominated two large buildings across the street that further anchored the business district: the ten-story Drexel Building (1888), the city's largest office building at the time, and The Bourse (1895). Nearby could also be found a cluster of the major cultural institutions: the Library Company, American Philosophical Society, Mercantile Library, Franklin Institute, and the Athenaeum.[6]

In the 1880s and 1890s, however, the entire business district drifted farther west toward Broad Street, pulled by several landmark buildings. In 1871 the city committed to build its new City Hall on the ten-acre square that William Penn had set aside for "Buildings of Publick Concerns" at Broad and Market. When Alexander Milne Calder's statue of William Penn was hoisted to the top of City Hall in 1894, it became the tallest building in the world, announcing to all that Philadelphia was one of the world's great and powerful

City Hall, in the foreground of this photograph taken circa 1920, was finally completed in 1904, with considerable cost overruns. The statue of William Penn, by Alexander Milne Calder, at 548 feet, remained the tallest feature of the skyline until 1986. Across from City Hall was the Broad Street Station of the Pennsylvania Railroad. The train shed, so massive that it became known as the "Chinese Wall," ran west along Filbert Street (now John F. Kennedy Boulevard). (Copyright © Terra Flight Aerial Services. *Free Library of Philadelphia*, Print and Picture Collection.)

cities. In 1881 the Pennsylvania Railroad, the nation's largest corporation, opened its Broad Street station and corporate headquarters directly across the street. An immense stone viaduct carried the trains west to the Schuylkill with low openings for the cross streets, creating such a formidable barrier to development north of Market Street that it became known as the "Chinese Wall." In 1893 the Reading Railroad opened its new terminal on East Market at Twelfth Street. A farmers' market that previously stood on the site found new space under the train shed at Twelfth and Arch, and, ironically, outlasted the terminal.[7]

In the same decades, a host of new technologies—structural steel, safety elevators, electric lighting, telephones, and typewriters—made it feasible to build tall office buildings for rapidly growing corporations and business firms. South Broad Street provided attractive sites for new office towers because the wide street meant ample light and air for high buildings as well as proximity to local government, the courts, and intercity rail service. Financial institutions, eager to impress the public with their wealth and strength, led the way. The eight-story Girard Trust Bank at Broad and Chestnut, built in 1890, although modest by later standards, was among the first commercial high buildings. By 1900 the seventeen-story Real Estate Trust Building and the twenty-two-story Land Title Building towered over the same intersection. During the next three decades, steel-frame office towers, mostly in the fifteen- to twenty-story range, rose in the immediate vicinity. In 1924 the Packard Building, at Fifteenth and Chestnut, set a new height of 324 feet. Philadelphia in the 1920s had a distinct skyline with the statue of William Penn at the pinnacle.

The post–Civil War decades also saw the emergence of the department store, featuring open displays, a single price for everyone, credit, free home delivery, a generous return policy, and the convenience of a wide range of merchandise under a single roof. By the early twentieth century, the city's five largest, lining East Market Street—Lit Brothers, Strawbridge and Clothier, Gimbel Brothers, N. Snellenburg, and John Wanamaker—became great civic landmarks. Wanamaker, who began his career at thirteen as a store clerk, emerged as one of the nation's premier retailers by offering customers a full guarantee and cash refunds and attracting attention with men carrying sand-wich boards on the sidewalks and billboard-covered wagons roaming the streets. In 1875 he purchased the vacated Pennsylvania Railroad freight depot at Thirteenth Street, added a false façade with towers and Gothic windows, and called it Wanamaker's Grand Depot. In 1912, Wanamaker rebuilt the store in a neo-Renaissance style. It occupied a full square block and featured a dramatic atrium, the Grand Court, with an enormous pipe organ, giving it a cathedral-like quality. Organ concerts and elaborate holiday pageants soon became a local tradition. A cast-iron eagle, purchased from the 1904 St. Louis World's Fair and installed on the ground floor, became the store's symbol and a Philadelphia icon.[8]

The enlarged downtown also developed distinct entertainment zones. Vaudeville theaters, with live acts suitable for the entire family, clustered on Chestnut, Walnut, and Arch Streets. In the 1920s four new large stage the-aters—the Schubert, the Erlanger, the Forrest, and the New Locust—made the city a popular site for tryouts of Broadway plays, and several ornate "first run" movie palaces opened in the same area. East of Broad along Race and Vine Streets one could find other diversions: a busy "red light" district offer-ing burlesque halls and prostitution, gambling, and other illicit vices. Several theaters catered exclusively to African Americans, who were excluded from or relegated to the balconies of mainstream venues.[9]

The city's major mass-retailing department stores lined East Market Street between Seventh and Thirteenth Streets. This view looks west from Seventh Street. The cast-iron façade of Lit Brothers is on the right; across Eighth Street was Strawbridge and Clothier (later rebuilt as a larger store). Gimbel Brothers is on the left side of Market Street. This 1911 photograph also shows the evolving transportation modes: the Lit Brothers canopy announces the entrance to the new subway; horse-drawn wagons and streetcars fill the street; automobiles are parked in front of Strawbridge's and Gimbels in the middle distance. (William Rau and the Library Company of Philadelphia.)

By 1900, Center City had assumed the appearance and form it would retain for much of the century. People from across the region flocked there for the shows, movies, and parades, the stores and restaurants, and sometimes the vices as well. Going downtown was special; people dressed up for the occasion and pedestrians thronged the streets. Parents took their children to the department stores for holiday clothing, to visit Santa Claus, and to view the decorated windows. For those in a hurry there were Horn and Hardart Automats, with the dishes displayed behind little glass windows; the customer dropped in a few nickels, twisted a handle, and the window popped opened. Eliminating waitress service, the Automats were the original fast-food restaurants.[10]

The size and location of Fairmount Park also shaped the city. In the late 1860s, to protect the water supply and enhance "the health and enjoyment of the people," the state enlarged the park on both sides of the Schuylkill and extended it to include the Wissahickon Creek valley to the city's border; at twenty-seven hundred acres, it was the country's largest urban park. The state also established the Fairmount Park Commission. After 1900 the commission and an affiliated private group of elite citizens, the City Parks Association (CPA), founded in 1888, mobilized civic groups to promote acquisition of new parklands and once again encourage philanthropists to acquire and donate parcels. As a result, in short order the commission acquired Bartram's Garden in West Philadelphia, the nation's oldest arboretum, and parks in Germantown, Overbrook, Olney, Juniata Park, the far end of South Philadelphia, and Mt. Airy. In 1916 the commission assumed management of Penn's original squares and Independence Square. In addition, the commission acquired the valleys of Cobbs, Pennypacker, and Tacony Creeks as sites for recreation, protecting them from industrial development and preserving their natural beauty.

Equally important, the commission and the CPA spearheaded the building of the Fairmount (later Benjamin Franklin) Parkway and Northeast (later Roosevelt) Boulevard. Coinciding with the nationwide City Beautiful movement to create impressive civic spaces, the CPA actively promoted a grand boulevard to link the park with City Hall. The Parkway, opened in 1918, provided an impressive motor entrance to the city center from the Northwest and the suburbs. At its western end, atop the old reservoir, stood the Philadelphia Museum of Art, three massive Greek temples in distinctive yellow sandstone completed in 1928. A cluster of civic buildings arose around Logan Square (reduced to a traffic circle): the Free Library (1927), the new Franklin Institute (1934), and the Board of Education (1943, now the Family Court House), which joined the earlier Academy of Natural Sciences (1874). Planners of the Parkway were inspired by the Champs-Élysées in Paris, but it failed as a pedestrian boulevard; merely to cross it on foot was daunting. Rather than street-level shops and cafes, apartment buildings eventually lined the roadway from Logan Circle to the Art Museum. Not until late in the twentieth century did the Parkway begin to fulfill its promise as a principal venue for civic celebrations and parades, and in good weather, a pleasant jogging route.[11]

The Fairmount Park Commission and the CPA also lobbied for Roosevelt Boulevard to link Tacony and Pennypack with Hunting and Fairmount Parks. The Boulevard, built in sections from 1903 to 1918, opened the previously remote Far Northeast to settlement and thus played a critical role in the city's twentieth-century development. Meanwhile, in 1909, Mayor John Reyburn appointed a committee of businessmen to prepare a comprehensive city

The Northeast section of the city remained relatively inaccessible and undeveloped into the twentieth century. In this aerial view from 1927, Roosevelt Boulevard cuts across diagonally. Oxford Circle is at the lower left, and Castor Avenue runs straight north. (Copyright © Terra Flight Aerial Services. *Free Library of Philadelphia*, Print and Picture Collection.)

plan that led to the formation of an advisory planning committee in 1912. Although those initiatives went nowhere in the short run, tellingly, the proposals focused almost entirely on traffic and Center City, which remained the predominant emphasis of planning for almost the entire twentieth century.[12]

Life and Work in the Age of Industry

Philadelphia built its prosperity on the sweat and labor of a quarter million workers. For most, conditions remained hard and dangerous, with long hours for inadequate pay. In the early twentieth century, although average annual incomes rose modestly, the standard workweek was still fifty-five to fifty-eight hours. Inside factories, new technologies brought a modicum of improvement in working conditions. Electric lighting greatly improved illumination, but lint in the textile mills, smoke in the foundries, chemicals in dye houses and tanneries, exposed machinery, and soot everywhere took their toll on human health and life. An 1880 study concluded that a family of five needed at least $640 a year for a minimally decent standard of living, but skilled workers' average annual income in the 1880s was only about $578, while the unskilled managed on about $374. In addition, four severe business depressions between 1873 and 1921 brought widespread suffering. In the depression of 1893, Baldwin cut its workforce from five thousand to twenty-four hundred within four months, and the average weekly wage fell from $13.06 to $7.12. In the spring of 1914, one-quarter of the textile workers were unemployed. In years of hard times, the desperate had to turn to private charities since the city had eliminated all direct public assistance.

To make ends meet, wives and children frequently had to supplement family income. Among major industrial cities, Philadelphia families had the highest percentage of multiple wage earners. Women accounted for more than a quarter of the workforce, clustering in textiles, apparel, and domestic service. White women with employed husbands rarely worked outside the home, but single women living on their own or widows with children struggled to survive. Employers paid women much less than men regardless of the industry. However, beginning in the 1890s more white-collar opportunities, as teachers, nurses, secretaries, and retail clerks, opened for native-born women, including the daughters of immigrants. Most boys went to work at fourteen or fifteen and girls a year later. Children between the ages of twelve and seventeen constituted 15 percent of the workforce. About half labored in sweatshops and most others worked in textiles, where fully 25 percent of the workforce was under fifteen. Only in the 1910s did child labor begin to decline.[13]

The workers' standard of living was spartan. Diets relied heavily on meat and starches, with fruits and vegetables only in season and supplemented with canned tomatoes and peaches. Their small row houses rarely had central heat. Before World War I illumination was only by gas light, and only a minority had an icebox. Nevertheless, families had high rates of homeownership, which represented a considerable sacrifice for the entire family. Besides demonstrating a level of social status, homeownership could allow the family to take in boarders and provide security in old age. In 1910 a quarter of all families counted themselves homeowners; by 1930 half were homeowners, but with high mortgages.

Despite employers' hostility to unions and a pro-management local government, workers maintained a union tradition and occasionally went on strike against wage cuts and poor conditions. In 1869 a group of Philadelphia craftsmen founded the Knights of Labor. The Knights espoused a single union across gender, ethnic, craft, and even racial boundaries. The conservative national leadership opposed strikes, but just the idea of a union of all workers frightened employers, who worked to quash the movement. At the peak of its influence in the mid-1880s the Knights of Labor had upwards of three hundred locals in Philadelphia, mostly in garments and textiles, and 750,000 members nationally, but later in the decade it rapidly lost influence and membership.

Even where craftsmen maintained unions, formal bargaining was the exception. For example, in the textile mills, at the beginning of each season a delegation of workers would meet with the owner to discuss piece rates, and after agreement was reached the proprietor would initial the wage scale and post it in the mill. It was not considered a formal union contract, but it brought some stability to labor-management relations and preserved workers' sense of dignity. But workers, both men and women, also fought for their right to a decent livelihood. For example, in 1879–1880 and again in 1885 the women carpet weavers in Kensington engaged in prolonged strikes, demonstrating that women workers could be just as militant as men.[14]

Philadelphia had a reputation as strongly anti-union city. Employers effectively exploited workers' ethnic and racial differences to keep unions weak and maintained close ties to local politicians to ensure that the police and judges were on their side. Nevertheless, from the 1890s on the number and duration of strikes increased as inflation eroded wages. Tensions reached a climax in 1910 in two strikes. In the first, seven thousand young women, mostly Jewish immigrants who sewed shirtwaists (tailored women's blouses), demanded higher wages, improved working conditions, an end to sexual harassment by bosses, and union recognition. While the police protected strikebreakers, other unions provided support, as did many college and society women. The strikers, many of them in their teens, showed extraordinary discipline and picketed through a bitterly cold winter. The strike dragged on until February when the manufacturers agreed to the women's demands, including union recognition. This settlement came in the midst of an even larger strike by streetcar workers after the Philadelphia Rapid Transit Company (PRT) fired all its employees who joined a new union and imported strikebreakers to maintain operations. Mayor John Reyburn deployed the police to protect PRT property as mobs of enraged workers in Kensington attacked the streetcars, breaking windows and disrupting service. On February 23, when a scuffle broke out along Broad Street, police fired into a crowd of Baldwin workers on their lunch break, causing a riot.[15]

During the streetcar strike of 1910, when thousands of workers walked out in support, the state sent in mounted police, ostensibly to maintain order, though the officers were clearly biased against the strikers. Here the state police, with clubs raised, chase a demonstrator up a front stoop. (*Free Library of Philadelphia*, Print and Picture Collection.)

Once peace was restored, the unions, leading newspapers, and many clergy called for arbitration, but the PRT, backed by Reyburn, determined to smash the union. The entire Pennsylvania mounted police force rode into town, patrolling Kensington and Frankford, breaking up demonstrations and liberally busting heads. Labor leaders called for a citywide general strike in support and within days more than a hundred thousand people had walked off their jobs in the largest display of worker solidarity since 1835. The partial general strike and widespread antipathy toward the company forced a compromise settlement, with workers winning most of their demands but not union recognition. Twenty-nine deaths were attributed to the strike, about half resulting from accidents caused by inexperienced car drivers.[16]

To insure workers' loyalty and lure them away from unions, large firms, such as John B. Stetson Company, Henry Disston and Sons, and John Wanamaker, pioneered welfare programs and better working conditions. They provided and sponsored social clubs, bands, night schools, sports teams, health programs, vacations, and even profit sharing. Disston gave workers low-interest loans to buy houses. Known collectively as welfare capitalism, those programs were popular with employees, but they rarely extended down to the thousands of smaller mills and shops where the majority of people worked.[17]

Meanwhile, immigrants kept coming. In 1910, 60 percent of Philadelphians were either immigrants or their U.S.-born children. Despite the large numbers, however, Philadelphia had a smaller overall share of immigrants than did comparable large cities for several reasons. The anti-Catholic riots of the 1840s had discouraged Irish settlement. Later, immigrants did not want to compete with the city's African American population for unskilled jobs, and, after the turn of the century, midwestern cities, with their assembly-line production, offered more opportunities for unskilled workers. But percentages can also be deceptive: in 1910 Philadelphia had more people of Irish ancestry than Boston, more Germans than St. Louis or Detroit, and more Italians and Jews than any other city except New York.[18]

Until the 1890s most immigrants came from Ireland, Britain, and Germany. Southwark, Moyamensing, and Gray's Ferry, all near the Delaware or Schuylkill waterfronts, had strong Irish communities, Germans were heavily represented in Northern Liberties and Kensington, and the textile mills of Kensington, Manayunk, Germantown, and Frankford were magnets for English immigrants. Beginning in the 1880s the sources of immigration shifted as thousands of Jewish, Italian, and Slavic people poured in, often via the Washington Avenue Immigration Station maintained by the Pennsylvania Railroad. Jews and Italians found small, established communities that provided some grudging assistance; but, within both communities, the newcomers, with their European folkways, embarrassed the earlier arrivals. Whereas the German Jews had gone to great lengths to acculturate and followed the liberal Reform movement, the Polish and Russian newcomers persisted in traditional Orthodox practices. The Irish-dominated Catholic Church considered Italian religious practices to border on the pagan.[19]

The labor preferences of different groups also influenced their location. East European Jews arrived with extensive experience in trades and commerce. They avoided factories, but many quickly gravitated to the garment industry, which became the largest employer of Jewish immigrants. They clustered predominantly in Southwark and South Philadelphia, where they found an ample supply of old cheap housing and proximity to the garment industry. A small colony of northern Italian immigrants at Eighth and Christian Streets became the nucleus for the large migration from southern Italy and Sicily. Many of the earlier settlers were craftsmen, while later arrivals went to work in construction or food handling. Because they preferred to work outdoors and with fellow countrymen, Italians avoided heavy factory labor and came to dominate public construction and street work. They also

Among the worst forms of slum housing were damp below-grade cellar apartments, such as the one shown here. This 1902 photograph was taken by the Philadelphia Housing Association, which lobbied for improved housing conditions. (Special Collections Research Center, Temple University Libraries, Philadelphia, PA.)

worked in large numbers in the garment trades, with many women doing sewing in their homes.

The shops along Ninth Street between Catherine and Federal became the nucleus of the Italian Market, famous for year-round fresh produce and imported Italian specialties. Slavic immigrants were drawn to heavy industries, such as iron and steel mills, chemical plants, and slaughterhouses, where the pay was relatively good but the conditions hard. They established communities in Bridesburg, Richmond, Nicetown, and Manayunk. A tiny but visible Chinese community emerged around Ninth and Race Streets. Most Chinese worked in laundries and restaurants around the city but gravitated to Chinatown for companionship. Immigration restrictions kept the community small until the 1940s.[20]

No group dominated any neighborhood, but while immigrants might rub shoulders with other people in the streets, in their social, cultural, and spiritual lives they kept to themselves. Clustering eased acculturation for immigrants who spoke little or no English, sought familiar foods, and relied on word-of-mouth to find work. Religion provided a primary outlet for spiritual solace and ethnic solidarity. Every community built elaborate houses of worship that announced their presence and laid claim to their turf. Each group also established lodges, social clubs, mutual insurance funds, and building and loan associations. These institutions often drew on immigrants from a particular province or even a single village. At one time the Italian community supported more than four hundred such organizations. The larger groups had their own foreign-language newspapers.[21]

In the 1920s federal quotas brought European immigration to a virtual halt. The 1930 census revealed that six hundred thousand Philadelphians, almost one-third of the population, were either foreign born or second generation. The Irish still made up the largest segment, at about a quarter of the total; East European Jews and Italians each accounted for about 20 percent; Germans and the British (English, Scottish, and Welsh) another 15 percent each. The immigrants and their children struggled to achieve a solid financial footing. Discrimination, especially against Italian, Jewish, Chinese, and Slavic groups, limited job and school opportunities. With considerable sacrifice, some saved to buy a house, while others put their faith in education for the next generation.

Not all newcomers, however, came from abroad; the city also attracted increasing numbers of African Americans, mostly from the upper South. By 1900 the community had grown to sixty-two thousand, even before migration surged in response to World War I labor shortages, and migration continued at a high level through the 1920s. African Americans continued to struggle for dignity and recognition of their legal rights. During the Civil War, their exclusion from the city's new streetcar system led to humiliating incidents, prompting a civil rights movement led by Octavius Catto, a gifted teacher at the Quaker-run Institute for Colored Youth. After passage of the Fourteenth Amendment in 1870, federal troops had to be called out to prevent violence when blacks tried to vote for the first time since 1838. In the 1871 elections, with no troops present, white mobs, supported by the police, tried again to block blacks from voting. Catto was killed on election day, but not in the rioting; rather, he was targeted and assassinated for his leadership role. His death was a grievous loss to the community.[22]

Most African Americans could find work in only stereotypical service jobs that paid the lowest of all wages and eroded a person's dignity. In 1880, 60 percent of black men and 90 percent of black women were employed as domestics or service workers, compared with about 30 percent of immigrants and less than 10 percent of native-born whites. When African American men managed to secure a toehold in manufacturing, it was usually in the dirtiest and least desirable jobs. Nonetheless, such jobs provided better pay than service work. On the eve of World War I, black male workers made fertilizer, printing ink, bricks and cement, and iron and steel forgings. They paved streets, maintained railroad tracks, and worked in construction and along the waterfront. Black barbers, caterers, coachmen, hotel workers, and construction laborers had their own unions, but the skilled trades unions refused to accept black members. The rare exception was the longshoremen of the radical Industrial Workers of the World, which maintained a strong integrated union from 1913 to 1922. Black women, far more likely to work than white women, still toiled almost exclusively in low-wage domestic and service jobs.[23]

Despite their poverty, segregation, and oppression, African Americans supported a rich communal life with their own institutions to nurture self-expression and leadership. State law kept the public schools segregated from 1854 to 1881, but even after the law changed they remained largely segregated by custom. In predominantly African American neighborhoods, black children attended separate schools with black teachers, often in decrepit buildings with gas lights and outdoor privies. In this context, the churches continued to provide the vital functions of fellowship and consolation. As the largest black-owned venues, they doubled as concert and meeting halls. There were also numerous black lodges and all-black building and loan associations. The weekly *Philadelphia Tribune*, begun in 1881, provided news and an autonomous voice. White philanthropic support made possible schools, hospitals, and asylums for the aged, orphaned, and infirm. The refusal of white hospitals to allow black physicians to practice in their facilities led to the establishment of the Frederick Douglass Memorial Hospital in 1895 at Sixteenth and Lombard.[24]

At the turn of the century, African Americans clustered in a highly segregated district between Spruce and Fitzwater, west of Seventh Street. The neighborhood was convenient to the mansions of Rittenhouse Square, where many found employment as domestics. With decent housing always scarce, and even harder to find during World War I, those who could afford to sought out better homes in nearby all-white areas. But when a black family attempted to move into the Gray's Ferry neighborhood in June 1918, a four-day riot ensued, with whites attacking blacks, who received little police protection. Some black families succeeded in securing a foothold in white neighborhoods, but when they did, whites generally fled, so that the level of segregation actually increased. In virtually all instances, blacks moved into older houses because no one in the 1920s would sell them new houses. By 1930 African Americans were more

In an era before movies and radio, people made their own entertainment. Music groups were popular among individuals of all backgrounds. Pictured here is the African American Treble Clef Old String Orchestra, circa 1905. (Sullivan Studio and the Library Company of Philadelphia.)

heavily segregated than they had been a decade earlier; most lived in slum housing and suffered high incidents of disease and premature death.[25]

While fewer in number than the industrial workers, the nonmanual middle-class workforce expanded rapidly after the Civil War. The best paid included professionals, successful businessmen, and corporate executives, mostly middle-aged, native-born white men. Below them in income were the growing numbers of middle managers and supervisors, shop owners, salesmen and agents, educators, artists, and musicians. Almost all were men, but beginning in the 1890s, more white-collar opportunities opened for women, primarily as office secretaries or retail clerks, but also in lower-paid professions such as teaching and nursing. What all middle-class workers had in common was clean work, a steady job with little fear of seasonal layoffs, and after the turn of the century, even a vacation. In 1900 about one-third of families could be considered middle class, probably more by aspiration; by 1929 this proportion had risen to almost 40 percent.[26]

The streetcars and commuter rail lines enabled middle-class families to create residential neighborhoods away from the noise and dirt of the factories and the immigrants. In West Philadelphia, for example, a middle-class residential neighborhood emerged after 1858 when horsecar service extended across the river. The electric trolley and commuter rail lines opened still more land, first to middle-class families and later to successful immigrants and skilled workers. In West Philadelphia, trolley service in the 1890s along Lancaster Pike and Haverford and Lansdown Avenues attracted new middle-class housing, and, after 1908, the Market Street Elevated brought the district within fifteen minutes of Center City. The neighborhoods of Mill Creek, Haddington, and Hestonville rapidly filled with two-story brick row houses with front porches. In the 1910s and 1920s, successful Jewish and Italian immigrants and African Americans moved into the area. Much of North Philadelphia, Tioga, and Germantown, which one historian called "a bastion of the bourgeoisie," also filled with substantial houses, many semi-detached or single family.[27]

Strawberry Mansion, typical of many pre–World War I streetcar neighborhoods, provided a more modest residential alternative for the lower-middle-class and successful artisans. The row houses, built almost entirely in the 1890s, fronted on the sidewalk, but some had bay windows and porches. Although the area offered little employment, it enjoyed excellent trolley service to Kensington and Center City, making it desirable for families with multiple wage-earners. In 1900, most residents claimed an Irish, German, or English background; about two-thirds of the family heads worked as skilled craftsmen and another quarter as clerical workers. By the 1920s, Russian Jews displaced the earlier residents, but the class profile changed little.[28]

As always, the rich and upper middle classes had the most residential choices. After the Civil War, while established elites gravitated to the fashionable Rittenhouse Square, the new money industrialists erected handsome mansions along North Broad Street. Toward the end of the century, the well-off could commute to town by rail from several carefully planned city neighborhoods, notably Overbrook Farms and Chestnut Hill, or they could leave Philadelphia entirely for the suburban Main Line, a real estate venture of the Pennsylvania Railroad. Chestnut Hill lies ten miles from City Hall, in the far northwestern corner, beyond Germantown; railroad service reached the area in 1854. After Fairmount Park annexed the Wissahickon Creek valley in 1868, providing a buffer to preserve its bucolic character, the area attracted wealthy businessmen, who built large stone houses. In the 1880s and 1890s, the Chestnut Hill Improvement Association raised money to plant trees, pave and maintain sidewalks and streets, and even build a water reservoir. Thus, in the decades before any zoning laws, affluent residents were able to shape and control their environment.[29]

Politics and Culture in the Machine Era

In 1903, Lincoln Steffens, a leading national journalist, labeled Philadelphia the worst governed city in the United States, calling it "corrupt and contented." Kickbacks from city contractors, insider deals on real estate, and outright bribery financed the activities of a Republican political organization that was powerful at the local, state, and national levels. The Progressive-era reform mayor Rudolph Blankenburg called it a "pernicious machine, which, well-greased, runs smoothly and unchecked on the highway of vice, graft and civic demoralization." City workers were expected to contribute 3 to 12 percent of their salary to the party, while a corrupt election process provided myriad opportunities to insure the selection of loyal men. More than once ballot boxes ended up in the river. The party, like similar organizations in other cities, attracted immigrant voters by providing ad hoc welfare, dispensing patronage jobs, ensuring that the police largely ignored regulations on liquor sales, and buying votes for a dollar each. From 1887 to 1933, with only two exceptions (1905 and 1911), the Republicans won virtually all city and county offices, leaving Democrats so weak by the 1920s that Republicans were secretly paying the rent on their party's office to maintain the semblance of opposition.[30]

The consequence of an entrenched machine with no check on its abuses was a poorly run city and a neglected infrastructure, sometimes with tragic cost. The management of basic utilities laid bare the cost of corruption. After the Civil War the city extended gas service, but the Republican boss James McManes used the city-owned gas works as a source of patronage to build the party organization, leaving the city with inferior service and high prices. Finally, in 1897, while retaining ownership, the city leased the gas works to a private firm in exchange for a flat rental fee. Meanwhile, the city dragged its feet on installing water and sewer mains, delayed constructing additional reservoirs, ignored warnings of deteriorating water quality, and rejected proposals for water-filtration plants. The bosses provided monopoly franchises to the streetcar and later rapid-transit syndicate led by the well-connected partners Peter Widener and William Elkins that meant inferior and overpriced service.[31]

Philadelphia's corruption was not unique, nor was it always the most egregious, but by World War I other large cities did better in all those areas. The city could have ensured that its water was drinkable and that all houses had an indoor water tap and a toilet connected to the sewers. It could have improved surface drainage to eliminate stagnant water and keep basements dry, and it could have cleaned its streets regularly and provided more playgrounds in the immigrant neighborhoods. For example, in 1913, when the state finally passed a housing act to outlaw the worst slum conditions, city council, beholden to real estate interests, refused to fund the necessary inspectors. The Republican machine neglected the public schools, which were so overcrowded in the early twentieth century that one-third of the pupils attended only a half day, while, despite compulsory attendance laws, another thousand children waited for room to enroll. A 1921 state report labeled the school buildings "deplorable," with "unwholesome" bathrooms.[32]

Although undoubtedly corrupt, the city was not content. At least some of the social and business elites organized ostensibly nonpartisan groups, such as the Reform Club and the Committee of Seventy, to elect honest and efficient officials. But the reformers had little broad-based appeal; they were wealthy men who spoke mostly with one another and made little attempt to reach out to immigrants and workers. They usually expressed more interest in cutting taxes than in spending more effectively to address pressing public needs. Men dependent on municipal jobs had little interest in cost-cutting schemes. The reformers were offended by the blatant corruption and concerned about the poor living conditions, but they did not like politics. They could not bring themselves to engage in the nitty-gritty work of building coalitions and creating an effective counterorganization. Furthermore, they were solidly Republican, firmly committed to the conventional high-tariff orthodoxy, which made it difficult to build alliances with the Democrats.[33]

Before the 1930s, the reformers' only victory came in 1911 when a factional struggle within the political machine enabled the Quaker merchant and longtime reformer Blankenburg to narrowly capture the mayor's office. Although the machine kept firm control of the city council, the Blankenburg administration demonstrated what an honest and capable government could achieve. Under the leadership of Morris L. Cooke, an engineer, the city undertook overdue and badly needed improvements: it eliminated railroad crossings at street level; introduced some efficiency in the fire, police, and sanitation departments; started construction of the Frankford Elevated (Frankford El) and North Broad Street subway; erected new piers; and increased school spending by 60 percent. Cooke fired hundreds of political functionaries who did no work and hired trained engineers and other professionals. Unfortunately, Blankenburg was self-righteous and politically naive. He refused to use patronage to reward his supporters or build a durable independent organization to compete with the machine. When he vetoed a bill to reduce gas rates, breaking a campaign promise, he lost considerable support. In 1915, the machine regained the mayor's office with a weak and pliable candidate whose tenure involved more scandal.[34]

In the new century, the construction contractors George, Edwin, and William Vare of South Philadelphia and "Sunny Jim" McNichol from North Philadelphia controlled powerful factions within the Republican machine. Together they garnered most of the lucrative city contracts and did extensive work for the local utilities, the telephone company, and the Pennsylvania Railroad, with the excess costs funding the machine's activities and lining their pockets. They built the Market Street subway, Roosevelt Boulevard, the Parkway, and the Torresdale filtration plant, with a cost overrun of about one-third. In 1926, William Vare won a U.S. Senate race with a huge margin in the city. But rumors of widespread fraud led to a Senate investigation that uncovered twenty-five thousand phony voter registrations (including large numbers of the deceased, ineligible recent immigrants, and children), along with multiple voting, stuffed ballot boxes, and false counts. The Senate refused to seat Vare, who died soon after.

Despite the sordid politics, Philadelphians managed to build civic institutions that enriched the community, uplifted its spirit, and created enduring legacies for future generations in the fine arts and culture. In some instances, however, complacency and conservatism limited the achievements. Cultural conservatism and social snobbery cost the Philadelphia Museum of Art several fine private collections, including the industrialist Albert Barnes's magnificent Impressionist and Post-Impressionist collection, for which he built his own private gallery in the suburbs. Similarly, the Philadelphia Orchestra, founded in 1900, enjoyed national prestige and represented the city's greatest achievement in the arts. But there, too, the conservative tastes of the local elites often clashed with the brilliant Leopold Stokowski, director from 1912 to 1936, who introduced most of the twentieth century's finest composers to the city and the country but was eased out after 1936. Finally, despite the founding of the Free Library in the 1890s as a result of the receipt of several large gifts, including one by the streetcar baron Peter Widener for a million dollars, not until 1927 did Philadelphians construct a public library building worthy of the city's size and wealth.[35]

For the majority of the people, however, the fine arts held little interest. In the late nineteenth century, people mostly made their own entertainment. The middle class formed singing societies, mandolin groups, and hiking and bicycling clubs; they played chess and parlor games and read aloud. Those who could afford it might ride an open streetcar to cool off or take an excursion train to Atlantic City, while hundreds of thousands flocked to Fairmount Park for picnics, promenades, and carriage and sleigh rides, and for skating, sledding, boating, and team sports. Rowing along the Schuylkill River became exceedingly popular with elegant boathouses lining the east bank. But the park was not accessible to everyone. For the burgeoning immigrant communities in South Philadelphia, Kensington, or Richmond, a park visit meant a streetcar ride, a prohibitive expense for struggling families except on special occasions. There was little open space in the most densely populated neighborhoods except for the streets.[36]

Particularly after 1900, better pay and shorter hours provided more working-class residents the means and opportunity to patronize commercial entertainments. Vaudeville and minstrel shows enjoyed wide popularity, with performers wearing blackface, reinforcing every vicious stereotype of African Americans. Professional baseball also gained a following in 1882, with the formation of the American Association Athletics and the National League Phillies the following year. Under the leadership of Connie Mack, between 1901 and 1931 the Athletics won nine league championships and five World Series. In 1909, the Athletics moved into the thirty-five-thousand-seat Shibe Park (later, Connie Mack Stadium) at Twenty-First Street and Lehigh Avenue. The Phillies, playing at the inferior Baker Bowl at Broad and Lehigh, struggled as the second-tier team and won a single pennant, in 1915, but lost the World Series. By the 1920s people of all classes followed the teams, but for many in the working class, ticket prices and daytime games precluded their attending. For the children of the immigrants, however, to play and follow baseball was to embrace American culture.[37]

The outbreak of World War I in 1914 boosted the economy with thousands of jobs and new residents. Local firms supplied Britain and France with enormous quantities of arms and other war materiel. When the United States entered the war in 1917, the large Ford plant at Broad and Lehigh stamped out infantry helmets, while Stetson made hats and caps for the army. Seven miles south of Center City, at Hog Island, the federal government's Emergency Fleet Corporation hastily erected an enormous facility at which seventeen thousand workers constructed more than three hundred ships. Large numbers of men and materiel were shipped out of the port to Europe. Wartime production created a great shortage of workers, exacerbated because the war cut off European immigration and the draft drew off thousands of local young men to fight. Domestic migration to the city resulted in a population jump of 6 percent between 1915 and 1919 and an acute housing shortage. The federal government built six hundred well-planned houses around Tenth Street and Oregon Avenue in South Philadelphia for Navy Yard workers, and

Philadelphia's row houses spread for miles in every direction and anchored its strong neighborhoods. Before the Civil War, narrow houses—mostly two stories—opened directly onto the sidewalk. In the late nineteenth and throughout the twentieth centuries, wider houses with modest setbacks—such as the houses in this 1924 photograph of Lycoming Street near O Street, in the Juniata section—featured front porches and bay windows. (Library Company of Philadelphia.)

the Emergency Fleet Corporation built another two hundred houses around Elmwood Avenue in the southwestern section of the city before the war ended.[38]

During World War I the federal government offered labor unions unprecedented support in order to maintain war production, resulting in a surge in union membership. After the war, unions attempted to solidify those gains, but the government pulled back its support and most of the strikes failed. Organized labor, in Philadelphia and elsewhere, faced a fundamental structural problem. Large employers had deep pockets and enjoyed the support of newspapers, the courts, and government officials at all levels in any serious showdown with the unions. In contrast, skilled workers had organized themselves along craft lines, so that in any given firm literally dozens of different trades unions made cooperation difficult. Further, the conservative unions, dominated by white men, made little effort to reach out to women, recent immigrants, African Americans, or the unskilled generally, all of whom they disdained as inferior. Under such conditions, it was unlikely unions could make much headway. Strikes, like the one at Cramp's shipyards in 1921, had virtually no chance of succeeding.[39]

Despite the erosion of the unions, the 1920s was a decade of prosperity for many. Thousands of families purchased automobiles, radios, and appliances (usually on credit) and bought the new row houses and twins spreading around the city's edges, made more accessible by Roosevelt Boulevard, the Frankford El (1922), and the North Broad Street subway (1928). New factories opened in electronics, radios, and automobile parts, particularly in West and Southwest Philadelphia and north of Lehigh Avenue. Yet, Philadelphia was in trouble. The formula of diversity and innovation that had served the local economy well for so long was no longer working. Its largest industries were obsolete, and the new products of assembly-line manufacturing concentrated elsewhere. Cramp's shipyards built several luxury liners after the war but closed in 1927. In 1906, Baldwin began to shift operations south of the city to Eddystone, and in 1928, closed the Broad Street works. Although full-fashion hosiery bolstered the textile industry, total employment peaked in 1925 as the industry shifted production to outlying towns and the South, where employers paid workers less and more easily fought off unions. In April 1929, even before the Great Depression, unemployment in Philadelphia stood at 10 percent, and half of those people were idle more than six months. The sluggish economy, combined with a cut-off in foreign immigration and out-migration to the nearby suburban towns, led to a population increase in the decade of only 7 percent, the lowest rate of growth to date.[40]

During the 1920s African Americans continued to pour into the city. Although blacks now found employment with the railroads and in manufacturing, their jobs paid little. The family income of unskilled black male workers varied little from that of unskilled whites, but only because more black wives and children contributed to family income. The historic black ghetto just south of Center City spread east into blocks Jews and Italians were abandoning and expanded in sections of North and West Philadelphia. A 1924 survey of recent migrants indicated that, despite widespread racism in the city, the greater freedom of movement and treatment in public compared with conditions in the South was a great source of satisfaction. But the poor, both black and white, still often lived in houses lacking indoor toilets, running water, and central heat. Little was done in the decade to address those conditions.[41]

The twenties also brought Prohibition. Local politicians had little stomach for it, refusing to enlarge the police department or support a crackdown on violations. Mayor Freeland Kendrick appointed marine general Smedley Butler to clean up the city, but his raids on speakeasies and private homes met with widespread opposition. Butler tried, unsuccessfully, to break up the cozy relationship among the police, ward politicians, and the local courts that protected the illicit drinking. After two years the mayor fired Butler. A 1928 national magazine article reported that the city tolerated 1,185 open bars and

13,000 speakeasies, each paying a weekly bribe to the police and lenient judges. Prohibition, in Philadelphia as elsewhere, provided fertile ground for organized crime, which took strong hold in parts of South Philadelphia and long outlasted the repeal of Prohibition.[42]

In the decade the city went on a building binge, financed almost entirely by bonds, because the business and commercial leaders stopped fighting the political machine and united around a range of projects to reduce the density of population, improve public health, and encourage homeownership: extension of water, sewer, and gas lines, new schools, and new rapid-transit lines. The elites spearheaded completion of such projects as the Free Library, the Museum of Art, and a municipal stadium. Hoping to repeat the success of the centennial celebration, businessmen and politicians also joined forces to host the Sesquicentennial International Exposition in 1926. Built on swamp land in far South Philadelphia (now the site of the sports arenas), it was a costly financial failure. In the long run, the city's investment in draining the swamp land and extending sewer and water lines stimulated development of the area, but in the short run, the city spent almost ten million dollars it could ill afford. The elites hoped those projects would bolster the city's image and make it attractive to new firms and thus offset declining industries. They turned a willful blind eye to the cost overruns and kickbacks that went with machine control.[43]

FROM THE CIVIL WAR to the Great Depression Philadelphia grew enormously and provided employment and housing to hundreds of thousands. The wealth generated provided private philanthropists with the resources to create a better community by investing in efforts to preserve open land and build important cultural institutions. After 1900 the city made impressive investments in infrastructure to open new neighborhoods and reduce density, but those gains came with the sacrifices of workers and immigrants who struggled to survive on inadequate incomes. While some businessmen tried to take on the political machine, too many tolerated the massive corruption and inept government. Other major cities had powerful and corrupt political machines but still managed to do better in meeting community needs.

4

ECONOMIC DECLINE/ COMMUNITY TURMOIL

1930–1980

IN ITS FIRST 250 YEARS, Philadelphia's size and wealth provided the city with the resources to shape its own destiny, but after 1930 everything changed. During the Great Depression Philadelphia's civic, industrial, and residential infrastructure deteriorated. In the decades after World War II much of the nation enjoyed tremendous prosperity, but not Philadelphia. The city's economic foundation and neighborhoods eroded while its suburbs boomed, and the city lost its dominance in the region. Civic leaders and everyday citizens took positive steps to halt the city's apparent decline and to control its future, but balancing those tensions became more difficult than ever.

Crisis in Peace and War: 1930–1945

The Great Depression fell on Philadelphia like a vast tornado, flattening almost everything in its way. From 1929 to 1933 overall business activity dropped by one-third, with manufacturing and construction the hardest hit. Hundreds of firms, large and small, closed down. At the low point, in March 1933, 40 percent of workers were idle, while another 20 percent worked only part-time. With rising unemployment homeowners fell behind on their loans, and a wave of foreclosures and evictions followed. From 1928 to 1932 almost 20 percent of owners lost their homes, a higher fraction than in any other city. Evicted families doubled up with friends or relatives, while homeless people erected shacks and shanties on vacant land, quickly dubbed "Hoovervilles" in derisive honor of the president. The largest encampment arose along

As the Great Depression worsened, thousands of people lost their homes. Many doubled up with relatives and friends, but others had to fend for themselves. Encampments of homeless people, mostly men, such as this camp of African Americans along the east bank of the Schuylkill River near the Art Museum, sprang up on vacant land throughout the city. These makeshift communities were often dubbed "Hooverville," after the president. (*Philadelphia Evening Bulletin*, July 2, 1932. Special Collections Research Center, Temple University Libraries, Philadelphia, PA.)

the east bank of the Schuylkill River just below the Art Museum. Waves of bank failures wiped out the savings of thousands. As the Depression worsened, soup kitchens and bread lines sprang up in missions, lodge halls, political clubs, and church basements, offering a hot meal with few questions asked. In working-class districts crowds harassed and sometimes chased away constables making evictions; large demonstrations of the unemployed at City Hall demanded work and food.[1]

The burden fell heaviest on factory workers, recent immigrants, the elderly, and African Americans, among whom the unemployment rate exceeded 50 percent. Even when the economy improved, discrimination blocked them from the few jobs available, so that by the end of the decade, blacks accounted for 60 percent of those eligible for work relief or public assistance. Women, too, carried a heavy burden. Most often it was they who applied for relief and struggled to keep discouraged husbands and hungry children together. The percentage of female workers rose because the economy provided more opportunities for service than for manufacturing jobs.[2]

In 1879 Philadelphia stopped providing relief to people in their homes, but the magnitude of the crisis quickly overwhelmed the extensive network of private charities. In November 1930, the mayor appointed H. Gates Lloyd, a socially prominent banker, to head a relief committee. The Lloyd Committee put together the nation's most comprehensive voluntary relief program. Families in need received vouchers redeemable at local stores for food or fuel. A school breakfast program fed ten thousand children; a citywide drive collected and distributed used clothing and shoes; a homeless shelter in the empty Baldwin factory housed twenty-five hundred men. In 1932 the city and the state, reluctantly, contributed to the effort, but at the end of June the Lloyd Committee was out of money and disbanded all its programs. By then it had turned over the hot breakfast program to the school board, closed the shelter, dropped the work program, and offered fifty-two thousand needy families only milk and flour. Voluntary private relief, a long Philadelphia tradition, had collapsed. Although many business leaders still opposed publicly-funded aid, the state established the County Emergency Relief Board, and in September assistance returned, after a lapse of ten weeks.[3]

The inauguration of Franklin D. Roosevelt in March 1933 ushered in a series of New Deal programs that included relief for the destitute, jobs for the unemployed, and assistance to homeowners facing foreclosure. Philadelphia desperately needed investment in its infrastructure, but the Republican machine and the business community bore such hostility to the New Deal that the city at first refused to participate in public employment programs because politicians feared loss of control over patronage to Democrats, which could undermine the machine. At one point New Deal officials sent Philadelphia residents outside the city to work. Not until 1935, under the newly elected Republican mayor S. Davis Wilson, a former Democrat, did Philadelphia pursue federal dollars.[4]

The New Deal also sought to address the dismal housing conditions with programs to demolish slums and build affordable housing. In 1937, with strong support from labor unions, social welfare advocates, and the black community, all key elements of the New Deal coalition, the city established the Philadelphia Housing Authority (PHA) to take advantage of the federal public housing program. During the next four years the PHA constructed several large housing complexes, but it struggled with two issues that would plague public housing for decades: suitable locations and racial segregation. Of the three initial projects, the Tasker Homes in South Philadelphia sat on a former garbage dump next to an oil refinery, and the James Weldon Johnson Homes on a former cemetery. The Richard Allen Homes required the

The earliest public housing projects, which were all racially segregated, carefully screened tenants and provided such amenities as communal gardens. This June 1949 photograph shows the James Weldon Johnson Homes at Twenty-Seventh and Norris Streets. (Special Collections Research Center, Temple University Libraries, Philadelphia, PA.)

demolition of more than a thousand houses in lower North Philadelphia, most in wretched condition. All were segregated—Tasker for whites, Johnson and Allen for African Americans.[5]

The New Deal dealt more generously with homeowners. The federal Home Owners' Loan Corporation refinanced mortgages, spreading out payments for families struggling to keep their properties and saving fifteen thousand homes from foreclosure. Italian, Jewish, and black families in modest row houses benefited the most. Ten percent of all loans went to African Americans, who represented only 3 percent of homeowners. But the agency reinforced patterns of segregation by avoiding loans to African Americans in integrated neighborhoods.[6]

Other initiatives aimed to help workers on the job. The National Industrial Recovery Act of 1933 affirmed workers' right to organize, and the National Labor Relations Act of 1935 (Wagner Act) created a permanent enforcement agency, the National Labor Relations Board. Galvanized by those laws and supported by the newly formed Congress of Industrial Organizations (CIO), workers took control of their destiny as never before in a surge of labor militancy. The most dramatic strike began in January 1937, when more than a thousand workers at two plants of Electric Storage and Battery (Exide) staged a sit-down strike: they stopped working but refused to leave the plant. Critically, a sympathetic Mayor Wilson made sure the police kept order but made no effort to evict the workers. After six weeks Exide granted the workers a raise and a week's paid vacation, and the strikers marched out jubilantly. The following year, in a rare display of interracial solidarity, trash collectors and street cleaners went on strike and violence erupted, but the workers won. By the 1940s two-thirds of the city's workers belonged to unions. After World War II about 90 percent of production workers were unionized.[7]

Finally, the upheaval of the 1930s sowed the seeds for a dramatic, though somewhat delayed, change in municipal politics. In 1933, Wilson, then a Democrat running on a fusion ticket with Independent Republicans, narrowly won election as controller along with candidates for city treasurer and magistrates over the Republican machine candidate. Meanwhile, the building contractors John B. Kelly and Matthew McCloskey worked with the real estate developer Albert Greenfield and the city's labor leaders to rebuild the Democratic Party. They found a strong base among factory workers and reached out to African Americans who had historically voted Republican. Those groups became key constituencies in a revived Democratic Party. In 1935, Wilson sought the Democratic nomination for mayor, but Kelly wanted the nod. Rebuffed, Wilson switched parties, won, and kept the Republicans in control of the city council. Although Roosevelt carried the city by an astounding two hundred thousand votes in the 1936 presidential race, the Democrats split into factions, enabling a revived Republican organization to maintain its hold on city government for another fifteen years.[8]

The city government had few resources with which to combat suffering or hire the unemployed. Almost all city revenue came from property taxes, and the steep drop in values undermined the budget. Mayor Wilson cut the real estate tax, an extremely popular measure that, nonetheless, only aggravated the city's precarious finances: interest payments consumed more than half of city revenue. In 1938, under heavy pressure from bankers, the city council passed a 2 percent sales tax, and the following year, it imposed a 1.5 percent income tax on wages, salaries, and profits, payable not only by residents but also by nonresidents who worked in the city. It was the first local income tax in the nation, and it tapped the suburban commuters to share the costs of running the city.[9]

It took World War II to restore prosperity. The city contributed enormously to the war effort. Federal defense spending rose with the outbreak of war in Europe in September 1939 and surged the following year. The Baldwin plant reopened and began to roll out thousands of tanks, diesel engines, and locomotives. Cramp's built warships, the Budd Company made aircraft parts, Brill made gun carriages, Disston rolled light armor plate, Philco made radar bombsights, and Rohm and Haas made bomber noses. More than fifty thousand people repaired and built ships at the Navy Yard, while twenty thousand produced an avalanche of weapons at the Frankford arsenal. The textile and apparel industries turned out coats, uniforms, blankets, parachutes, and a host of other goods. Stetson alone employed five thousand people making hats. And, out of sight, a team of engineers at the University of Pennsylvania, under an army contract, developed ENIAC, the first prototype computer.[10]

By 1942, unemployment had disappeared and a critical manpower shortage drew in thousands of newcomers, especially African Americans from the South and small numbers of Puerto Ricans. Many manufacturers hired blacks for the first time, partly because of pressure from the federal government. But longstanding racial antipathies remained. The depth of race prejudice was laid bare in August 1944 when the Philadelphia Transportation Company, under pressure from black activists and the federal government, agreed to hire African American streetcar motormen and conductors. Most white workers walked out in a hate strike, although the Transit Workers Union that represented the workers and supported interracial unionism opposed it. The company helped to foment the hate strike in order to divide the workers and undermine the union. The city barely averted a full-scale race riot as white gangs marauded through black neighborhoods. Meanwhile, neither the mayor nor the governor made any effort to dampen racial tensions or mediate the dispute. With people unable to get to work, war production dropped immediately. After four days, the federal government seized the company and threatened to draft any worker who stayed out. The army sent five thousand soldiers, who rode the cars for ten days while calm was restored, but the ugly episode boded ill for postwar race relations.[11]

The war also opened new opportunities for women as employers recruited them for jobs previously considered "men's work," including welding, riveting, and operating lathes and presses. By 1944, 35 percent of women had gainful employment and constituted 40 percent of manufacturing workers.

With the severe labor shortage during World War II, the government aggressively recruited women for factory work, as it had in World War I. The title of the February 1942 *Philadelphia Bulletin* article that accompanied this photograph of women running grinding machines was "Outdoing Men at Masculine Jobs." (Special Collections Research Center, Temple University Libraries, Philadelphia, PA.)

Women gained more visibility in politics as election-day volunteers, replacing men now in uniform, and they took an active part in administering and monitoring rationing and price controls. Women hosted the USO dances and receptions that provided diversion for soldiers and sailors.[12]

The war ended the Depression and restored the nation's self-confidence. It created a sense of common purpose and enabled people of all ages to contribute to a cause larger than themselves. Children threw themselves into newspaper and scrap drives. When the city offered vacant land for "victory gardens," an estimated one hundred thousand families participated. Movie theaters, where attendance soared, sold war bonds and showed films that bolstered morale and delivered a message of personal sacrifice. The public endured rationing of essential foodstuffs and gasoline, although those willing and able to pay extra could buy rationed goods on the black market. People had cash in their pockets for the first time in years. In the summers they jammed excursion trains to the Jersey shore and the Poconos. More than 180,000 Philadelphians served in the armed forces; 5,000 did not return.

The "Philadelphia Renaissance" and "Urban Renewal"

By the end of the war, the decades of inefficiency, corruption, and neglect finally caught up with Philadelphia. With drinking water so odorous that people called it a "chlorine cocktail," raw sewage dumped in the rivers, horses still pulling garbage wagons, and streets lit with gaslights, Philadelphia ranked as the dirtiest city in the nation. Center City office space stood vacant; mass transit ridership declined, while automobiles clogged the narrow streets. Organized crime thrived, and Philadelphia's own *Saturday Evening Post* labeled the city "shabby." More ominously, the manufacturing sector began to decline and the population began to slip. Further, impoverished African Americans and Puerto Ricans arrived as affluent whites were departing, exacerbating racial tensions.[13]

To challenge the city's notorious lethargy and overturn the entrenched political machine would require bold leadership and an engaged citizenry. Beginning in the late 1930s a small group of socially prominent young professionals laid the groundwork for a civic revival, moving along two fronts simultaneously: rebuilding the Democratic Party and offering citizens a vision of a modern city. Using urban planning as a catalyst for change, they mobilized a broad coalition of civic organizations and labor unions to promote planning and to serve as a watchdog over city agencies. In addition, the business community finally realized how much corruption hurt the city's reputation. Borrowing a model from Pittsburgh, in 1948 a hundred influential men in law, banking, and insurance organized the Greater Philadelphia Movement (GPM) to address the city's problems. During the next twenty years the GPM played a key role in initiating and promoting political reforms and programs for economic revitalization.[14]

In 1951, the electorate, aroused by a succession of corruption scandals in which numerous officials went to jail and five committed suicide, approved a new city charter that streamlined government and finally established an effective civil service law. Then voters ended sixty-five years of Republican control, electing two young patrician lawyers, Democrats Joseph Clark as mayor and Richardson Dilworth as district attorney, along with fifteen other Democrats to the city council. In 1956 Dilworth succeeded Clark as mayor and served until 1962.

Clark's and Dilworth's efforts to revive the city drew national attention, and the press spoke of a "Philadelphia Renaissance." In the 1950s, when the city still had the resources to address its problems, it built new water and sewage treatment plants, bridges and schools, police and fire stations. It expanded the airport, fixed the streets, built new ones, modernized garbage collection, converted the Market Street Elevated to a subway, and purchased cars for the Locust Street line, built during the Depression but never opened. Although citywide infrastructure investment absorbed the bulk of capital spending, Center City attracted the most attention. Despite its seedy appearance, the business district remained strong. In 1955, more than six hundred thousand people worked there, and planners assumed it would remain the dominant shopping and employment center of the metropolitan region.[15]

A few years earlier, the City Planning Commission had captured the public's imagination and attracted national attention with the "Better Philadelphia" exhibit, which used dioramas and moving panels to demonstrate the potential of planning to revitalize the city. The "Philadelphia of Tomorrow" featured a business district with modern office buildings, a mall facing Independence Hall, and a rebuilt residential neighborhood near the waterfront. But it also proposed improvements throughout the city, such as playgrounds, health centers, and schools as well as a network of highways linking the Pennsylvania Turnpike to downtown and to the Industrial Highway along the Delaware River. The exhibition was principally the work of Edmund Bacon, who served as executive director of the City Planning Commission from 1949 to 1970. Although Bacon's interests were citywide, his biggest influence was on Center City. For the next half century the city's strategy for economic revival and the bulk of resources focused on Center City.[16]

In the 1950s, three major projects, Independence Hall historic district, Penn Center, and Society Hill, established the parameters for the modern downtown. Despite its rich collection of historic sites, Philadelphia was not a very attractive tourist destination. Parking around the historic district was scarce, and the buildings were poorly marked and deteriorating. In the 1950s, the state demolished three square blocks—Chestnut to Race between Fifth and Sixth Streets—for Independence Mall, and the National Park Service

---

Facing page: This 1967 City Planning Commission map shows the Center City Redevelopment plans. Some of the projects took decades to complete. Key: 1 = Penn's Landing; 2 = Delaware Expressway (I-95); 3 = Society Hill; 4 = Independence Mall; 5 = Vine Street Expressway (I-676); 6 = East Market Street Gallery; 7 = Crosstown Expressway along South Street (never built); 8 = Penn Center. (Philadelphia City Planning Commission, *Center City Redevelopment Area Plan* [Philadelphia, 1967].)

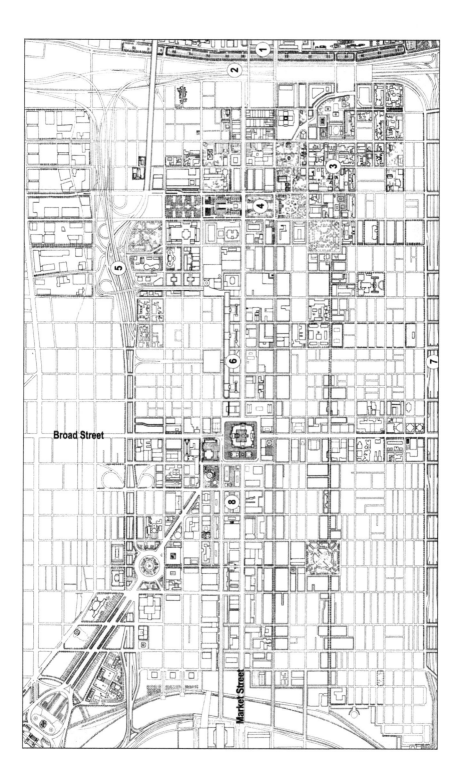

Broad Street

Market Street

cleared the three blocks to the east for Independence National Historic Park, including numerous historic nineteenth-century buildings along Chestnut Street, despite the strenuous objections of Bacon and others. The mall was largely a failure: it overwhelmed the modest Independence Hall, it trampled on Penn's orderly grid, and it was too large and windswept to attract strollers. Three massive federal buildings, a court house, the Federal Reserve Bank, and the Mint, presented bleak façades to the mall. Bacon hoped that office buildings with street-level shops generating pedestrian traffic would line it, but only a few such places materialized. Tourists instead gravitated south along Chestnut Street to the Visitors Center at Third Street, opened in 1976, and to the shops and restaurants of Society Hill.[17]

At the other end of Center City, in the early 1950s, the Pennsylvania Railroad demolished its Broad Street Station and the massive viaduct known as the "Chinese Wall," providing a rare opportunity to reshape the heart of the business district. Bacon envisioned a project similar to New York's Rockefeller Center, but the Pennsylvania Railroad owned the property, so he could only cajole and implore. He named the project Penn Center, but the railroad's priority was maximizing its investment rather than creating a landmark. The resulting buildings were banal and the below-ground space cramped and uninviting. But by opening the area west of City Hall to new development, Penn Center marked the beginning of downtown revival. Unfortunately, the flawed plan missed an opportunity for a truly striking design.[18]

For the third prong of Center City revitalization, Bacon targeted an area of mixed commercial activity and deteriorated housing east of Seventh Street and south of Walnut. Mostly poor residents occupied the neighborhood, but it possessed several important attributes: close proximity to Center City offices, a large stock of eighteenth-century townhouses, and several historic structures. Bacon used historic preservation as a strategy for redevelopment, reviving the colonial designation Society Hill since it was originally developed by the Free Society of Traders. The city created several quasi-public corporations that could arrange private financing but would have full governmental power of eminent

Facing page, top: Mid-twentieth-century Independence Hall, in the foreground of this view to the north, was hemmed in by nineteenth-century office buildings. (Harry S. Hood and the Library Company of Philadelphia.)

Facing page, bottom: This 1987 photograph of the view north from Independence Hall shows Independence Mall between Fifth and Sixth Streets from Chestnut to Race Streets. Lined with office buildings, the mall was relatively uninviting to tourists. In 2003 the Constitution Center opened on the block between Arch and Race Streets. (Susan Oyama and the Library Company of Philadelphia.)

After the Broad Street train station and the "Chinese Wall" finally came down in the early 1950s, the Pennsylvania Railroad built the Penn Center office complex. This view toward the southwest shows City Hall in the lower left and the Penn Center buildings under construction. The parking lot in front of City Hall is now Dilworth Park. The first block of Benjamin Franklin Parkway, in the lower right, is now JFK Plaza (also known as Love Park). (Copyright © Terra Flight Aerial Services. Library Company of Philadelphia.)

domain. The first corporation, the Food Distribution Center, acquired city land in South Philadelphia, where it relocated the food distribution markets. This move opened the way for a private developer, with federal subsidies, to build three, thirty-story luxury apartment buildings that became known as Society Hill Towers. Meanwhile, a parallel entity, the Old Philadelphia Development Corporation (OPDC), working closely with the city, used eminent domain to condemn virtually all Society Hill properties. Critics later considered it a naked transfer of poor people's land to the well-off, although, except for the residents, it raised little controversy at the time. The OPDC allowed current owners to stay in their homes only if they had the willingness and resources to renovate them in conformity with historic guidelines; otherwise OPDC sold the houses to new buyers who agreed to restoration along strict historic guidelines. Not all buyers were residents; many were investors who purchased properties at bargain prices, undertook the renovations, and then resold the houses for a substantial profit. When Mayor Dilworth and C. Jared Ingersoll, a socially prominent banker and a leader in the GPM, moved to the area, others were encouraged to follow, and by the mid-1960s a critical mass of newcomers had arrived and the anticipated transition was well under way. By 1980, Society Hill was a neighborhood of the high-income college-educated class. The value of owner-occupied houses was seven times the citywide median.

Widely applauded at the time and hailed as a model for what later became known as gentrification, remaking Society Hill nevertheless entailed very real human costs. Although Bacon, GPM businessmen, and investors saw only a slum, the area was a genuine neighborhood with dozens of local businesses and a dense social network of lower-income but working-class residents. The OPDC forced out six thousand people, many with just two months' notice, including homeowners who lacked the aspiration or resources to renovate and tenants, who were just evicted. Shopkeepers lost their businesses with little compensation and less sympathy. Unlike many areas in other cities where urban renewal projects were undertaken, the Society Hill neighborhood was not simply bulldozed. To those who were displaced, however, the difference was inconsequential.[19]

Meanwhile, to encourage the revival of deteriorated downtowns, in 1949 Congress established an urban renewal program that provided subsidies for cities to acquire slums and resell the land to private developers at one-third of the cost. The Philadelphia program was run by the Redevelopment Authority, which, in the 1950s, using its eminent domain power, acquired a wide swath of lower North Philadelphia, an overwhelmingly black and Puerto Rican area, evicting thousands of people and businesses and destroying whole neighbor-hoods. It assumed that real estate just north of the business district, once cleared, would attract private developers. But developers failed to rush in. Some blocks lay vacant for decades, accumulating trash and contributing to the sense of desolation. In addition, the local universities, especially the University of Pennsylvania (Penn), hemmed in by their surrounding neighborhoods, turned for help to city officials who were eager to cooperate because they saw the schools as sources for economic development and bulwarks against the spread of "blight." In the 1950s and 1960s the Redevelopment Authority cleared block after block for the expansion of Penn and other schools, and state and federal renewal funds subsidized construction of new campus buildings. In the black community, urban renewal came to be known as "Negro removal."[20]

The largest urban renewal project, in the city and the nation, was in East-wick, the low-lying area in far Southwest Philadelphia. In 1950, nineteen thousand people lived there in scattered neighborhoods. The city had long neglected the area, so it lacked sewers, paved streets, and streetlights, and some of the housing was in deteriorated condition. Yet 72 percent of families owned their homes, and it was a rare racially integrated community. Once again, in making grandiose plans to redevelop the area, the planners failed to see a thriving neighborhood of modest-income families. In the 1950s, over residents' vehement protests, the Redevelopment Authority took possession of the entire area and evicted thousands of people for a large-scale project of new neighborhoods and industrial parks. Planners wanted Eastwick to be integrated, and so they stalled selling or renting to black families until they secured a minimum number of white families. Despite being blatantly illegal, the scheme received the tacit approval of the city. Eventually the new Eastwick was a success. It provided a substantial stock of modest-income housing, and its proximity to the airport and the Interstate network enabled it to attract industrial and commercial firms that provided employment. In the late twentieth century, it was again an integrated neighborhood, about half white and half black, although by 2014 most of the area was predominantly black and included a cluster of recent immigrants from West Africa.[21]

In contrast to many other public needs, when it came to professional sports, the city eagerly invested scarce capital. Sports provided at least some commonality to the diverse and fragmented population, although team executives were often indifferent to broader community desires. By the 1950s the city's sports facilities were inadequate and obsolete. The Phillies played at Connie Mack Stadium in the middle of an increasingly impoverished neighborhood with no parking, while the Eagles played at Penn's Franklin Field. To hold onto its teams, the city built the Spectrum for hockey and basketball and Veterans Stadium (the "Vet") for the Phillies and Eagles, both in South Philadelphia on land reclaimed for the 1926 Sesquicentennial International Exposition. Despite the expense, neither facility was entirely satisfactory, however, and the city was still paying off bonds for the Vet after it was demolished in 2004.[22]

Deindustrialization and Suburbanization

For 150 years manufacturing had propelled Philadelphia's economy, providing its citizens, in 1950, with 350,000 industrial jobs. But during the subsequent half century Philadelphia lost its manufacturing base; it deindustrialized. Numerous factors accounted for the decline. Assembly-line production, located elsewhere, displaced the skill-based, flexible manufacturing that characterized Philadelphia industry. Technological innovation eliminated many jobs. National and international corporations acquired many local firms and, lacking any particular commitment to Philadelphia, made decisions about capital investment that took no notice of social or economic costs, turning to

Deindustrialization hollowed out neighborhoods and the industrial district. While some old buildings in Center City and Manayunk were remodeled as lofts, most abandoned factories stood derelict, such as the building in this 2016 photograph, located on Master Street between American Street and Germantown Avenue in Kensington. (Author's collection.)

the South and later abroad for cheaper, non-union labor. The federal government encouraged siting new defense plants in the South and West. Labor relations were mired in hostility. And the city's industrial infrastructure was old and obsolete. Nineteenth-century mill buildings in dense neighborhoods stood along narrow streets and railroad sidings, but increasingly business needed wide streets with ample loading docks. Suburban towns built industrial parks around highway interchanges, where light manufacturing and warehousing could find exactly the kind of space it needed.[23]

From 1957 to 1970 alone the city lost 75 percent of its manufacturing jobs. A few product lines—chemicals, machinery, pharmaceuticals, and electrical and transportation equipment—at first offset the steep drop in the city's bulwarks of textiles, apparel, and metalworking, but the bleeding of jobs soon became a hemorrhage Philadelphia could not stanch. By the 1960s such major employers as Midvale Steel, the Budd Company, Philco Radio, and the Stetson Company had either sharply retrenched or closed down.[24]

Although those developments reflected national and global trends, Philadelphia made an effort to control its destiny, working aggressively to hold and attract employment. It sponsored fifteen industrial parks and was the first city in the country to use public land for such purposes. In 1958 the city chartered a mixed public-private corporation, the Philadelphia Industrial Development Corporation (PIDC), to acquire sites and finance new factories. The PIDC developed eight major industrial parks, the largest two surrounding Northeast Philadelphia Airport and Eastwick in the southwestern part of the city. It also facilitated the relocation of firms displaced by urban renewal and highway projects. But many of their sites were not served by public transportation and were thus inaccessible to inner-city residents. Beginning in the 1970s, PIDC provided financing for many inner-city industrial and commercial projects as it broadened its mission to include more concern with social issues. Overall, PIDC played an important role in efforts to retain and attract jobs within the city and contributed substantially to the city's tax base. It could not stop deindustrialization, but it saved some jobs.[25]

As manufacturing declined, so did the port. The piers could not handle newer container ships and trucks could not maneuver in the narrow streets near the waterfront. The port was slow to adopt cost-saving measures to handle containerized cargo, and, in 1960, Los Angeles surpassed Philadelphia as the nation's third largest port. The Port Corporation, established in 1965, modernized facilities for container cargos and opened new marine terminals, but it was insufficient. Only political influence kept the Navy Yard open until the 1990s. By 2014 the port had fallen to thirty-fifth in total tonnage.[26]

By the late 1970s the city had more service than manufacturing jobs. The service economy covered a wide range of activities and occupations. The largest sectors were wholesale and retail trade, hospitality, health care, education, government (federal, state, local), banking, and insurance. Service occupations ran the gamut from minimum-wage hotel maids and retail clerks to physicians, lawyers, bankers, and executives, but many of the best-paying office jobs went to suburban commuters. When laid-off factory workers found new jobs, the pay was often lower and the benefits few. In 1980 the employment rate for the city was 11.4 percent, 50 percent higher than the region's.[27]

Deindustrialization did not affect everyone equally. Particularly in the quarter century after 1945, strong economic growth and powerful labor unions raised the standard of living of most white citizens. After fifteen years of depression and war, families were eager for the new homes, cars, and appliances promised in wartime advertising. In those years, thousands of families purchased new homes, many of them semi-detached and single-family houses, all along the city's periphery, primarily in Oak Lane, Cedarbrook, Roxborough, Wynnefield, Overbrook, and the entire Northeast. Between 1940 and 1970 the number of housing units jumped 26 percent.[28]

Even more people left the city entirely, however, driving in their new cars to the adjacent counties where builders created a suburban environment of single-family houses on large lots. Suburbanization was not inevitable; rather it was the outcome of explicit state and federal housing, zoning, and transportation policies. Federal mortgage-insurance programs and income tax policies kept mortgage costs low and made owning cheaper than renting. In a practice known as redlining, federal agencies and banks discriminated against the older, high-density communities that characterized almost the entire city. They rarely insured loans for home improvement in older neighborhoods and, most perniciously, flatly rejected applications from African Americans, who were forced to pay higher interest rates when they could get mortgages at all. Racial discrimination in the sale or rental of real estate was not illegal until 1968 and remained pervasive even afterward. Further, suburban residents used zoning ordinances to create homogeneously affluent white communities by banning apartments or even modest single homes on small lots. Property taxes were low because suburbanites did not share the high costs of social welfare and education for Philadelphia's increasingly impoverished citizens.[29]

Highways also literally paved the way to the suburbs. The state highway department, dominated by suburban and rural interests, laid out the routes and subsidized state roads while the federal government paid 90 percent of the cost of the Interstate Highway System. In the 1950s the Northeast Extension of the Pennsylvania Turnpike and the Schuylkill Expressway opened vast stretches of Montgomery County for suburban tract housing. In addition, the turnpike extension to the New Jersey Turnpike, combined with the Walt Whitman and Commodore Barry Bridges, the Mid-County Expressway (I-476), and I-295 in New Jersey, created an outer beltway surrounding Philadelphia. In contrast, the federal government provided no money for railroad modernization or urban mass transit until the early 1960s, and even then the amounts were paltry compared with the vast sums expended on highways.

As affluent consumers gravitated to the suburbs, planners, politicians, and backers of the GPM all assumed the city's survival depended on good automobile access for suburbanites. Between 1948 and 1955 automobile traffic in Center City doubled, aggravating congestion and parking woes in the narrow streets. A 1955 transportation study called for a coordinated regional network that included improved commuter rail and rapid-transit service as well as expressways. Although the report recognized that mass transit accounted for 70 percent of downtown rush hour trips, perversely it called for a highway loop encircling Center City. The federal Interstate Highway Act of 1956, providing 90 percent funding, made this ambitious scheme possible. The Schuylkill Expressway, linking the Pennsylvania Turnpike at King of Prussia to Center City, was the first segment of this loop. The route, following the west bank of the Schuylkill River and running through Fairmount Park, represented a difficult trade-off. Unlike expressways in other cities, it did not require that any neighborhoods be demolished to build it, but it cut the park off from the river and proved to be an engineering disaster, with dangerously sharp turns and short exit ramps from both left and right lanes. On its opening day in 1958, volume exceeded designed capacity, and soon there were so many fatal accidents that drivers nicknamed it the "Surekill."[30]

Other highway segments did require demolition of neighborhoods and generated considerable resistance. Plans for the Delaware Expressway (I-95) along the waterfront called for an elevated highway connecting the port and airport to the south with industry to the north. Residents of adjacent neighborhoods protested vigorously, notably the affluent homeowners of Society Hill. The compromise, supported by Bacon, was a below grade, partially covered roadway through Center City protecting Society Hill. But in adjacent Southwark, the route required razing 131 historic structures and separating a neighborhood of longshoremen from the waterfront. A plan to shift the route to save the homes was ignored.

In the 1950s, Vine Street was widened as part of the Center City loop and a submerged roadway built from Seventeenth Street to the Expressway, but completion of the eastern segment dragged on until 1991 because of the need to preserve Franklin Square and opposition to ripping apart Chinatown. The southern link, labeled the Crosstown Expressway, would have required demolition of the historic core of the African American community, which in the 1950s still featured a thriving jazz and club scene west of Broad Street. By the late 1960s, however, both nationally and locally, residents began to challenge neighborhood demolition for highways. A grass-roots alliance united opponents to the scheme—affluent white residents of Society Hill and Southwark with blacks living along the corridor. As pressure mounted, politicians hesitated. Finally, in the mid-1970s the whole project was canceled, but in the meantime, businesses, expecting demolition, had vacated South Street, causing property values to decline. In the mid-1960s, artists, galleries, boutiques, and cafes began to move into the eastern end, laying the basis for its revival as the epicenter of Philadelphia's vibrant bohemian counterculture.[31]

Despite all the attention to highways, Clark and Dilworth lobbied for mass transit aid. Under Dilworth the city took over the local transit company and obtained subsidies for suburban commuter lines, which led to a dramatic jump in ridership. In 1964 the state established the Southeastern Pennsylvania Transportation Authority (SEPTA) to coordinate regional mass transit. In 1968 SEPTA took control of the entire city transportation and suburban rail networks. But the suburban counties dominated the SEPTA board and never demonstrated much interest in doing what was best for the city. Nonetheless, Philadelphia remained far more reliant on mass transit than most other large cities.[32]

The shift in the locus of population and jobs created a wholly new urban form: the metropolitan region. The suburbs became self-sustaining economic units because most people who lived in the suburban counties also worked, shopped, and spent their leisure time there. By the 1980s, "edge cities" emerged at the confluence of major highways, notably at King of Prussia, Willow Grove, and Cherry Hill, New Jersey, where defense industries and firms in computers, instruments, and pharmaceuticals clustered with shopping malls and office buildings. A sporting event, parade, concert, or plane trip might bring suburbanites across the city line, but otherwise there was little need or interest in venturing into Philadelphia. While the city had more people, jobs, and retail sales than any single suburban county, its dominance declined by every measure. In 1930 two-thirds of the region's population lived in Philadelphia; by 1960, a majority lived in the seven surrounding counties; and in 1980, almost two-thirds. In 1980, only 26 percent of Delaware County residents and 18 percent from Montgomery County worked in the city.[33]

Racial Transition and Conflict

Philadelphia's population reached its all-time peak at 2.1 million in 1950, fell slowly during the next two decades, and then slid sharply to 1.69 million in 1980. While the white population rushed to the suburbs, the city continued to attract African Americans and Puerto Ricans. In 1950, 375,000 African Americans constituted 18 percent of the population; by 1980, 600,000 African Americans constituted almost 40 percent of the population. In 1980 the census also reported 63,000 Latinos, about 4 percent of the population, although that may have been an undercount.[34] In that process Philadelphia became poorer. From 1949 to 1979 household income of city residents fell from almost even with the regional median to only 73 percent. In 1980 unemployment among city residents was 50 percent higher than the regional average, and more than 20 percent of city residents struggled to survive on incomes below the official poverty level.[35]

When European immigrants settled in Philadelphia, the industrial sector was expanding and provided thousands of jobs for the unskilled. But as the black and Hispanic migrations peaked, deindustrialization accelerated. Most African American migrants had only a limited education, and Hispanics had little English facility. Both groups scratched out a living from minimum-wage marginal jobs others disdained. White workers held tenaciously to remaining well-paying jobs and resisted working alongside minorities. Many unions, particularly in the construction trades, refused to accept black members. Neither group had much access to the manufacturing jobs in suburban industrial parks even if firms would hire them. When the city proposed that SEPTA provide bus service from North Philadelphia to outlying industrial parks, the suburban counties rejected the idea. Blatant racial discrimination blocked entry-level service-sector positions that might lead to modest upward mobility. In 1970 the unemployment rate for African Americans was 50 percent higher than that of whites, and median income of black families was two-thirds that of all families. By the mid-1960s more than four thousand African American entrepreneurs owned a business, but most were small stores, restaurants, barbershops, or beauty parlors.[36] Custom and prejudice had confined Philadelphia's African American and Puerto Rican residents around the fringes of Center City where some of the oldest and worst slum housing could be found. In the 1940s, blacks clustered in three main areas: the historic ghetto south of Lombard Street and west of Seventh Street, lower North Philadelphia west of Ninth Street, and West Philadelphia between Market Street and Girard Avenue. The small Puerto Rican community concentrated west of Broad between Vine and Poplar. For both groups, continuing in-migration, particularly in the 1940s and 1950s when there was a severe housing shortage, aggravated existing overcrowding, leading to even further deterioration, as landlords subdivided the small row houses so that units often lacked separate kitchens and toilets, and even running water. Nevertheless, despite their low incomes, families in those neighborhoods nurtured social, religious, and communal institutions just as did other city neighborhoods.[37]

The flip side of remaking Center City was the undermining of those districts. In the 1950s and 1960s people evicted for highway, urban renewal, and public housing projects, having few options, crowded into adjacent blocks, where they usually paid higher rents. Consequently, those areas became overcrowded and deteriorated conditions spread farther. Many landlords neglected maintenance, collected as much rent as they could, stopped paying property taxes, and finally just abandoned their buildings. Between 1950 and 1980 a combination of arson, demolition, and abandonment swept away a stunning thirty-five thousand units in lower North Philadelphia, one-third of its total housing supply. Equally devastating was the loss of hundreds of small businesses. Displaced families qualified for public housing, but there was never enough of it; in 1954 the waiting list numbered seven thousand households.[38]

From the beginning, intense debates raged over the location of public housing projects. Planners identified vacant land in outlying areas where lower land costs would mean lower rents and larger apartments. Equally important, nobody would have to be displaced for construction. But whites who could not afford the suburbs staked their claim to the anticipated new housing and virulently resisted any public housing projects in "their," still-undeveloped, neighborhoods. Passions ran so high at a public hearing in 1956 that an irate white woman punched Mayor Dilworth in the nose. Advocates of public housing never intended it to be an arm of welfare, but strict federal income limits meant that the most successful and stable families had to leave, depriving the projects of role models and a leadership corps. In addition, redevelopment-initiated demolitions put increasing pressure on the PHA to admit displaced families that were often impoverished and otherwise disadvantaged. Consequently, 77 percent of the six thousand public housing units built from 1953 to 1961 were in high-rise buildings that reinforced racial segregation.[39]

African Americans in the rural South and Puerto Ricans had maintained strong kin networks despite their poverty, but circumstance in the urban North often weakened family ties. Because the men had difficulty securing even minimum-wage jobs, establishing and sustaining stable family relationships became harder. Although large numbers of women worked, women found it difficult to find marriage partners who could contribute support. (Federal programs gave more money to single mothers.) Black and Puerto Rican women often looked to Aid to Families with Dependent Children, known as welfare, and to public housing for help, but when they turned to those agencies they met resistance and sometimes humiliation. The city's welfare department was more interested in keeping down costs than in serving constituents. The programs lacked coordination and often reinforced the dependency they supposedly opposed.[40]

To address the paradox of persistent poverty amid national prosperity, in the 1960s the federal government launched a series of programs under the rubric of the War on Poverty that provided a variety of social services to the impoverished. While social services were sorely needed, the approach avoided confronting such intractable structural factors as discrimination in jobs, schools, and housing and the regional shifts in employment. Nonetheless, some of the initiatives made an important difference by providing preschool classes, day care, and health services to young children; repairing and building low-income housing and helping people attain mortgages; and offering legal aid to poor families. The federally funded social services provided white-collar job opportunities for many African Americans and lifted them into the middle class. In addition, the federal government's Medicare and Medicaid programs, providing medical insurance for the elderly and the poor, had an enormously positive effect on people's health. Many of the agencies running those programs continue to operate in the twenty-first century.[41]

Over the decades, Philadelphia became more segregated. Further, the combination of demolitions, high unemployment, low wages, and racial prejudice isolated African Americans and Puerto Ricans in neighborhoods characterized by dilapidated houses, widespread drug use, youth gangs (thirty-two in North Philadelphia alone), and rising street crime. As conditions in those areas deteriorated, upwardly mobile families sought better housing in less-congested neighborhoods that required crossing invisible, but very real, boundaries into white neighborhoods. Just as in earlier decades, the pioneers often met with fierce resistance.[42]

In working-class white neighborhoods such as Kensington, Bridesburg, and South Philadelphia, where social networks built around work, clubs, schools, parishes, and corner taverns reinforced a provincial, homogeneous white culture, residents lacked either the inclination or the resources to move and fought tenaciously to protect the homogeneity of their communities. For many whites, the greatest fear was a drop in property values, but this fear could become self-fulfilling. Unscrupulous realtors engaged in "block-busting": inducing panic selling among whites, then buying homes cheaply and reselling to African Americans and Puerto Ricans at higher prices.[43]

From the 1940s through the 1980s, although rarely reported in the major newspapers, vandalism, violence, even small riots along the shifting boundary lines of race became endemic as black and Puerto Rican families fought for decent housing. In the first half of 1955 alone, there were two hundred racial or ethnic riots, mostly involving whites and blacks. In a particularly nasty incident in October 1966, whites rioted for five nights in Fishtown when a black family moved in, and a crowd of 150, mostly teenagers, burned an African American effigy.[44] A rare exception was the upper-middle-class Mt. Airy section, where churches, synagogues, and liberal activists worked to build trust between white and African American families. They succeeded in driving out unscrupulous realtors and garnering scarce resources for their schools. For more than forty years West Mt. Airy remained a stable integrated, largely middle class neighborhood, although after the year 2000 segregation within the neighborhood became more pronounced. In the newest neighborhoods around the city's periphery, however, particularly the entire Northeast, as well as the suburbs, collusion among realtors, builders, and bankers kept those areas all white.[45]

African Americans moved into the nineteenth-century streetcar neighborhoods that never had a strong local employment base. In the 1940s, blacks in North Philadelphia moved north, staying west of Broad Street. In West Philadelphia, expansion spread south of West Market Street; in South Philadelphia movement was to the southwest, into Gray's Ferry and Point Breeze. The Puerto Rican community spread north between Germantown and Kensington Avenues from Northern Liberties to Roosevelt Boulevard in a narrow wedge between the black population in North Philadelphia and the working-class white population to the east. In 2010, Philadelphia was ranked as the fourth most segregated large city in the country.[46]

The pernicious effect of segregation is that it restricts opportunities for employment and for social advancement, especially in public education, and thus perpetuates inequality. Schools remained highly segregated, and minority students were often taught in old, dilapidated buildings by inexperienced teachers. For decades the Board of Education hid behind the rationale that segregation was only an outcome of housing patterns, although its policies purposely reinforced racial separation. In 1961 the local chapter of the National Association for the Advancement of Colored People filed a federal lawsuit to force desegregation, but it dragged on and on. A few years later, the city's Commission on Human Relations and the school board proposed a comprehensive busing plan for racial balance that met intense resistance, especially from the heavily white Northeast. The mayor slowed down implementation, and, after the Supreme Court rejected a Detroit plan for metropolitan-wide school busing in 1974, the incentive for busing in Philadelphia was severely reduced, since by then the student body was already majority black.[47]

Disillusioned by the slow progress on racial integration and economic opportunity, African Americans took charge of their condition in new ways. Although southern civil rights protests provided inspiration, the movement largely grew out of local conditions and was galvanized by the leadership of local black clergy, notably the Reverend Leon Sullivan, minister of the influential Zion Baptist Church in North Philadelphia. In 1960 the community launched a boycott of the prominent Tastykake Baking Company, demanding that it promote blacks into visible and better-paying positions. After two months, the company acceded to almost all the demands. During the next few years the movement negotiated agreements with several hundred firms and helped to widen good job opportunities for African Americans.

In 1963 Sullivan began an initiative that focused on providing training for specific jobs and combined it with remedial education and workplace social skills. By 1967, the program, known as the Opportunities Industrialization Centers, had a staff of sixty-eight serving more than nine thousand people. As black militancy escalated, white businessmen who had resented Sullivan's earlier boycott campaigns now saw him as a moderate and provided initial funding. Later the federal government provided most of its support and expanded the program to other cities, more than a hundred by the 1970s.[48]

Frustrated by the slow progress of racial integration, members of the local chapter of the National Association for the Advancement of Colored People (NAACP) picketed construction sites in the 1960s, demanding that all-white unions admit African Americans. These protesters are shown marching at a school construction site at Thirty-First and Dauphin Streets, in the Strawberry Mansion neighborhood, in 1963. (Special Collections Research Center, Temple University Libraries, Philadelphia, PA.)

Despite all those initiatives, in August 1964 accumulated frustration over pervasive racism and lack of progress on any meaningful changes erupted in a major race riot centered at Twenty-Second Street and Columbia Avenue (now Cecil B. Moore Avenue). Black rioters marauded through the neighborhood for three nights, looting and burning stores, but leaving most black-owned businesses unmolested. The police, under Commissioner Howard Leary, pursued a policy of minimizing injuries; consequently, there were only two deaths. After three nights the rioting dissipated, but the extensive damage accelerated the downward spiral of the district since most of the destroyed businesses never reopened.[49]

Through the rest of the century racial tensions remained high between blacks and the police, and occasionally between citizens directly. In 1970 police battled with the militant Black Panthers, and police commissioner Frank Rizzo called for machine guns and spoke of an insurrection. For more than a decade whites and blacks clashed in the Gray's Ferry section. In 1971 local whites threatened to form a vigilante group if police failed to protect them from black youth gangs. In 1979 two hundred whites tossed bottles and confronted a crowd of blacks while police tried to preserve order.

The Puerto Rican experience differed from the African American in some respects, although both groups suffered from the same structural problems. New black arrivals found an established network of churches and social service agencies. Puerto Ricans found only a small community of Spaniards and Cubans. Like all other immigrant groups, Puerto Ricans built their own institutions, churches, and beneficial organizations, notably the Council of Spanish Speaking Organizations (El Concilio) founded in 1962, and, in 1970, the Asociación Puertorriqueños en Marcha (Association of Puerto Ricans on the March, known as APM). The latter, an activist nonprofit agency, offered health, family, housing, and education services and affordable housing projects. Growing to ten locations, it became a major force in stabilizing Puerto Rican neighborhoods.[50]

In the 1960s and 1970s, with the population falling and the tax base eroding, the city strained to maintain essential services. In 1962 James H. J. Tate, the city's first Irish Catholic mayor, rose to prominence as a party functionary who struggled to balance the conflicting demands of the two key Democratic constituencies: the white working class and African Americans. Civil service reform under the 1951 charter had greatly reduced the number of patronage jobs, denying Tate the traditional leverage to hold factions together and deliver the votes necessary to win elections, and so Tate turned to the municipal unions. In 1967, facing a tight re-election battle against Republican district attorney Arlen Specter, he agreed to generous contracts with the city's workers. By then more than 40 percent of non-uniformed city workers were African American, and the contracts cemented their support. In one of the closest elections in the city's history, Tate won by ten thousand votes.[51] In 1965 the Philadelphia Federation of Teachers signed its first union contract, and in 1970, after a short strike, teachers earned substantial raises, further straining the city's finances.[52]

In 1972 Frank Rizzo succeeded Tate as mayor. An Italian American from South Philadelphia who dropped out of high school to join the police force, Rizzo first came to prominence in the late 1950s for arresting prostitutes and raiding gay bars, although he never showed much interest in pursuing gambling or organized crime. Rizzo was authoritarian by temperament and used aggressive police tactics, particularly against black demonstrators, making him an extremely polarizing figure and a hero for much of the white population. As mayor he fought a federal lawsuit against discrimination in the police department, tried to block a townhouse project for moderate-income families in the Whitman Park neighborhood, and resisted attempts at affirmative action in city contracts for black businesses and workers.[53]

During the Rizzo years the accumulating postwar trends converged to push the city into a rapid downward spiral. In the 1970s white flight took on the appearance of a stampede as the population dropped by more than 250,000, almost 14 percent. Manufacturing jobs fell 40 percent. Center City retailing experienced a sharp decline; in an ominous sign of things to come, Lit Brothers, a major department store, closed. Other numbers rose: taxes, crime rates, abandoned houses, and people on welfare—from 200,000 to 340,000.

Finally, a financial crisis building for years came to a head in the mid-1970s. The combination of generous union contracts, continued growth of the city workforce, declining tax revenues, cutbacks in federal aid, and surging inflation created a yawning deficit. Rizzo had refused to increase taxes during his first term, but, just after his reelection in 1975, property taxes jumped 30 percent and the payroll tax doubled. Rizzo sharply cut funds to social service agencies, including closing Philadelphia General Hospital, which had served the poor for almost two hundred years. Citizens saw a stunning physical deterioration in the city, particularly in the condition of the streets. But Rizzo managed to provide generous contracts to the mostly white policemen and firemen in a move that would plague city finances for decades.[54]

JUST AS THE CITY seemed at its low point, a 1976 feature film, *Rocky*, lifted its spirits. The film tells the story of Rocky Balboa, a small-time local boxer who is given the opportunity to fight the national champion. As Rocky trains for the fight, the movie shows him running through a gritty Philadelphia. The iconic scene is not the fight itself but the moment when Rocky, to the strains of inspiring music, dashes up the steps of the Art Museum and thrusts his arms in the air—a triumphal convergence of high art and popular culture. Today a statue of Rocky at those steps immortalizes the moment, and the image is an enduring symbol of Philadelphia.[55]

Philadelphia's challenges in the mid-twentieth century were similar to those faced by other large industrial cities. Since the cities borrowed ideas from one another, what one tried, others often copied.[56] Philadelphia got a few important things right, and in some instances became a model. It avoided ripping apart its business district for highways. It was in the forefront in developing public-private partnerships to attract private capital to redevelopment projects. It moved aggressively to hold industry in the city and to create neighborhoods attractive to affluent residents. Its growing black community initiated constructive measures to take control of its future. But the city struggled to meet basic community needs with a rapidly eroding tax base. The heightened racial tensions of the era made it difficult to build a citywide coalition for almost anything. Aid from the state was always grudging, and because Philadelphia is also a county it was burdened with high social service costs. Business leaders, who might have supported higher taxes for education and social spending, instead complained that the Philadelphia payroll tax and business taxes discouraged firms from locating in the city. In 1980 the outlook for the future did not appear promising.[57]

5

STRUGGLING TOWARD
THE POSTINDUSTRIAL CITY

1980–2016

IN THE LATE TWENTIETH and early twenty-first centuries, Philadelphia struggled to adjust to a postindustrial economy. The city no longer had the resources to invest in its future; it could barely maintain its infrastructure and provide basic services. A successful community required a prosperous economy, but a weak economy laid bare tensions between investing in social welfare and investing in economic development. Politicians, businessmen, civic leaders, and ordinary citizens all took steps to keep the city competitive in a new economic environment and to improve the quality of everyday life. But they faced daunting challenges, because, more than ever, much of the city's fate lay beyond their control.

The Politics of Decline and Remaking Center City

In the late twentieth century, deindustrialization and suburbanization continued to erode Philadelphia's population, economic base, and regional dominance. By the year 2000 the population had fallen to 1,517,000, a 25 percent drop in a half century, although other Rust Belt cities, such as Detroit, Cleveland, Pittsburgh, and St. Louis, had declined even more. After 2000 the population began to grow again modestly, reaching 1,567,000 in 2015. At the same time, manufacturing collapsed, its demise accelerated by free trade agreements and a flood of Asian imports: from 135,000 jobs in 1980 to 68,000 a decade later, and to only 21,000 in 2015. In 1996, two-thirds of all the land zoned for industry lay abandoned.[1]

Now white-collar services powered the economy, with health care and education the fastest-growing sectors, together employing more than one-third of the workforce. Hospitals and universities were the largest private employers. Finance, real estate, and information were the highest-paying sectors, although the number of jobs of those fields fell by over 40 percent from 1990 to 2014. Low-paying jobs in retailing and hospitality accounted for another 21 percent. Meanwhile, suburbanization continued to erode the city's position in the region. Less than 30 percent of the region's population lived in Philadelphia, and 37 percent of the city's labor force worked outside the city. In 2015 only three of the region's dozen Fortune 500 corporations had their headquarters inside the city.[2]

Job growth remained sluggish; between 1990 and 2013 total private sector jobs fell 6.8 percent. The best overall indicator of the impact of deindustrialization can be found in the unemployment rate. In 2000, almost 11 percent of city residents were unemployed, compared with 4.5 percent for the surrounding counties. The rate for African Americans and Latinos was 15 percent and 17.4 percent, respectively.[3]

At the same time, the state and federal governments demonstrated stunning indifference to urban problems. During the Reagan administration (1981–1989) direct federal aid to Philadelphia dropped from $250 million to $54 million. Ronald Reagan demonized welfare recipients and attacked labor unions. Pennsylvania also shortchanged the city, spending, for example, 50 percent more per capita in the suburbs than the city on highway construction and maintenance. Philadelphia's budgets revealed how the imbalance between city and suburb affected the quality of life and confounded efforts to balance the books. In the mid-1980s, compared with the suburbs, the city spent almost three times as much per capita on police, twice as much on recreation, and 50 percent more on sanitation, but less on its schools. The accumulating problems pushed up spending for social programs. For example, the state mandated new social services for neglected children but underfunded the reimbursement. What the city did have was the highest mass-transit fares and the highest rates of payroll tax, real estate transfer tax, and automobile insurance of any large U.S. city.[4]

The decline in employment, population, and federal aid eroded city revenue and led to chronic budget deficits that were exacerbated in the early 1980s by rising inflation and high interest rates. Finances preoccupied the two mayors of that decade, William ("Bill") Green III (1980–1984) and W. Wilson Goode (1984–1992), who struggled with the politics of declining resources. Green inherited a massive deficit from Rizzo and, compounding his problems, his term began during a sharp business recession. To build alliances with the black community, he appointed the African American community organizer

Wilson Goode to the powerful post of managing director. Together they cut city payrolls, raised taxes, endured a fifty-day teachers strike, and faced strike threats from the fire and police unions. Green's last budget showed a small surplus, but he suffered from an antagonistic relationship with the city council, which he labeled, with only moderate exaggeration, "the worst legislative body in the western world"—fistfights broke out on more than one occasion. Unfortunately, Green's relations with the press were not much better, and the mayor had no stomach for a second term.[5]

In 1983, Goode defeated Rizzo in a contentious Democratic primary and won election as the city's first African American mayor. Goode continued to streamline the bureaucracy and reduce government costs, and he cultivated good relations with the business community. Goode invested much of his attention and resources on Center City, but he also increased spending on programs for the poor, consequently running six consecutive budget deficits. He sought tax increases to close deficits, but a racially fragmented and corrupt city council balked. Meanwhile, the city's credit rating sank.[6]

Goode's most visible legacy was a low-budget program that attempted to combat the graffiti that seemed to be scrawled everywhere. The Philadelphia Anti-Graffiti Network enlisted a hundred young artists to create the "Life in the City" mural on the Spring Garden Bridge, which captured the city's attention and imagination. By 1991 there were hundreds of murals across the city. Reorganized as the Mural Arts Program, it turned the city into an art gallery. More important, mural projects built neighborhood cooperation and understanding and may have helped revitalize some neighborhoods.[7]

As mayor, Goode strove to reduce racial tensions and hired more blacks in government positions. So great was the racial polarization, however, that after his election politicians in the white Far Northeast advocated that the area secede from the city as a separate county.[8] Goode took steps to placate the Northeast, but deep-seated racial antipathies still flared up across the city. In 1985 when a mixed-race couple and a black couple bought homes in Elmwood, a working-class neighborhood of modest row houses in the southwestern part of the city, a crowd of four hundred whites appeared out front, pressuring the families to leave. The couples soon departed, but before they could remove their furniture, local teenage boys set one house on fire. The white families believed a conspiracy was afoot among the federal government, City Hall, and real estate interests to integrate their neighborhood. Similar ugly incidents flared when Puerto Ricans, Asians, and blacks pushed across invisible boundaries of race.

Under Goode's tenure Philadelphia endured its most bizarre and tragic episode. In the seventies a black radical fringe group called MOVE occupied

The 1985 police effort to dislodge the MOVE protesters from Osage Avenue resulted in a fire that destroyed sixty-one homes and all the residents' personal possessions. As this 2016 photograph shows, shoddy construction left many of the replacement homes unoccupied and boarded up. (Author's collection.)

a house in Powelton Village, creating an appalling nuisance by tossing garbage in the yard and shouting obscenities to harass their neighbors. In May 1978, police efforts to evict them led to a shoot-out in which one policeman was killed. In the mid-1980s a remnant of the group occupied a house on Osage Avenue in Cobbs Creek, a middle-class black neighborhood in West Philadelphia, and resumed their former behavior. When the police attempted to evict them, MOVE members opened fire and another siege ensued. The police, determined on revenge for the 1978 shooting, dropped a small incendiary device on the roof to smoke out the occupants, but it ignited a gasoline tank. The fire department delayed fighting the fire, which, before it could be controlled, destroyed sixty-one houses. Eleven MOVE members died, including five children, and the black neighbors who had called on the city to evict MOVE lost their homes.

Newspapers around the world carried pictures of a city bombing its own people. The episode further antagonized relations between the police and the African American community. Goode immediately promised to rebuild the destroyed homes but gave the contract to a crony. The saga of fraud and corruption dragged on for years. The new houses were so poorly constructed that in 2000 the city condemned them and planned, once again, to raze the block. In 2016 about half the replacement homes remained boarded up.[9]

The MOVE debacle undercut Goode's reputation, but the following year he won back some public support when municipal unions walked out on strike. Goode held firm against their demands while garbage rotted in the streets. After three weeks the unions settled, largely on Goode's terms. The following year Goode narrowly won re-election against now-Republican Frank Rizzo. The mayor tried to build support for a tax increase, but people wanted better services without higher taxes. In 1990, the country fell into another recession, unemployment shot up, revenues dropped sharply, and Philadelphia faced its worst budget crisis since the Depression.

No one did more to restore the city's confidence in itself than Edward ("Ed") Rendell, mayor from 1992 to 2000. With his ebullient personality he proved to be a relentless cheerleader for the city. In an aggressive public relations campaign he called on all constituencies to make sacrifices while depicting municipal unions as greedy and inefficient. When an agency created by the state to bail out the city proposed privatizing some city services, the prospect of large layoffs gave Rendell leverage to deal with unions. After submitting a credible five-year budget plan, rejecting further tax hikes, except for an increase in the sales tax, as job-killing measures, and bludgeoning the unions into accepting painful cuts, Rendell was able to stabilize the city's finances. Just as during the Great Depression, bond holders were paid in full while municipal workers and taxpayers bore the cost. Rendell also enjoyed good relations with the city council and worked closely with the African American council president John Street, who helped negotiate with the largely black non-uniform municipal workers and steered the budget plan through the city council. Rendell's mayoralty coincided with a period of strong economic growth, which, with his budget cuts, enabled him to deliver balanced budgets for the remainder of his term, giving him the credibility to lobby successfully for grants from the state and federal governments. For the first time in decades, residents and critics felt that the city might be able to handle its problems.[10]

Ever since the 1950s Philadelphia's mayors, planners, and business leaders viewed a Center City that could compete for white-collar businesses as the key to survival in a postindustrial service economy. The assumption, sometimes explicit, was that jobs and tax revenue would trickle down to the residents in the neighborhoods, although the best-paying jobs went mostly to suburban residents. In the 1980s and 1990s, the agenda to make Center City competitive included five major elements: improved commuter rail service, modern office buildings, a new convention center and hotels, a safe and vibrant downtown ambiance with attractive arts and recreational venues, and more gentrification. Those projects would require enormous private capital along with state and federal aid. To fulfill the agenda, the mayors cultivated close ties with the business community. In some ways the city acted as a real estate broker, assembling parcels the investors wanted for projects. But the city's revenue was so depleted and social needs so great that by the 1990s politicians had few options.[11]

The starting point was better rail service and new office space. In 1984, after long delays, a commuter rail tunnel, funded largely by the federal government, connected the Reading, Suburban, and Thirtieth Street Stations and made all parts of downtown accessible from disparate suburban towns. But commuter rail service remained inadequate for some time. The regional transportation agency, SEPTA, struggled through the late twentieth century, cutting service, raising fares, and suffering several strikes that did nothing to encourage firms to locate downtown. The rail link, however, made Market Street west of Broad more accessible and thus attractive for redevelopment. Within a decade a half dozen new office towers arose there, providing modern space for the rapidly expanding financial- and business-services sectors and creating a dramatic new skyline that signaled a dynamic city. The pinnacle was the sixty-one-story One Liberty Place at Seventeenth and Market Streets, which was developed by Willard Rouse III, a close friend of Goode's. The new structure generated considerable controversy because it exceeded by four hundred feet the informal height limit of William Penn's hat atop City Hall, but the glass-façade building quickly became the landmark feature of the new skyline. Since the new skyscrapers provided attractive, state-of-the art office space, some firms relocated from older downtown buildings. But suburban office employment grew faster, as firms repeatedly complained that high business and local income taxes made Center City uncompetitive.[12]

To compete for the large conventions that filled hotels and restaurants, the city needed a new hall to replace the obsolete and inaccessible Civic Center, but plans for a new facility generated enormous controversy. The city council opposed the construction of a new hall, justifiably arguing that it would do nothing for most Philadelphians, and their support was contingent on commitments for minority hiring in its construction. Built with a large state subsidy, the Pennsylvania Convention Center finally opened in 1993, located between Eleventh and Twelfth Streets from Arch to Race with the Market Street façade of the Reading Terminal as an entranceway. But controversy continued to plague it. High labor costs cut into bookings while other cities built larger facilities. In the new century, the state took control of the Convention Center and provided funds for expansion, but not until 2014 did the unions agree to greater flexibility on work rules to make the Convention Center competitive.[13]

To attract large conventions and lure new hotel construction the city needed a downtown area that was perceived as safe and attractive. As a start, Rendell initiated business improvement districts (BIDs), a concept already popular in several other cities. BIDs are private corporations with authority to tax local property owners to support a specific neighborhood district. In Philadelphia the Center City District (CCD) came first in 1991; it provided signage, security guards, street maintenance, and aggressive advocacy for downtown. CCD was a key step in Center City revival: its visible guards and staff gave shoppers, workers, residents, and tourists alike an enhanced sense of security. Meanwhile, the historic district received a much-needed facelift. In 2003 the National Constitution Center opened on the northern block of Independence Mall, facing Independence Hall. The new Visitors Center and Liberty Bell pavilion were built parallel to Sixth Street to avoid breaking the mall vista. The Bourse Building on Fifth Street was restored with restaurants and shops. With Independence Hall as the city's top attraction, tourism steadily increased.[14]

At the same time, artists and the business community, hoping to create a more welcoming environment for the arts, lobbied for a coherent cultural district along South Broad Street that came to be labeled the Avenue of the Arts. Rendell helped bring together a coalition of interested groups and raised money from corporations, developers, and the state. In the 1990s several new or renovated theaters opened, along with the relocated High School for the Creative and Performing Arts. The Kimmel Center, the visually stunning but acoustically uneven new home for the Philadelphia Orchestra, opened in 2001 at Broad and Spruce Streets. Overall, the Avenue of the Arts succeeded in stimulating a revival of South Broad with hotels, restaurants, and apartment houses. African American leaders hoped to extend the Avenue of the Arts along North Broad Street as a hub for black culture. The Freedom Theater at Broad near Master received a new building, but plans for other venues stalled. Clearly the bulk of money and interest gravitated to Center City. Furthermore, corporate support for the arts in Philadelphia overall lags behind the national average.[15]

Major league sports were far more important to most residents than cultural venues. Although the teams delivered few championships, they were a key marker of city identity, and fan loyalty was notoriously intense. By the late 1980s Veterans Stadium and the Spectrum, although hardly old, seemed inadequate, and the city faced the ignominious prospect of losing its teams. When the Flyers and 76ers threatened to move to New Jersey, Goode negotiated a deal to keep those teams in town, paying for infrastructure improvements while the Flyers partially financed the Wells Fargo Center, which opened in 1996.[16] The Eagles and Phillies also wanted their own stadiums. Rendell expended considerable energy searching for an acceptable location for a downtown baseball stadium, but the Phillies preferred highway access and parking for affluent suburban fans, and residential neighborhoods resisted a stadium. In the end both facilities went up at the south end of Broad Street. Lincoln Financial Field opened for football in 2003 and Citizens Bank Park for baseball the following year. The state, so stingy with Philadelphia in most matters, provided almost two hundred million dollars in subsidies, while the city chipped in another three hundred million, although critics questioned whether such wealthy businesses required any taxpayer subsidy. In exchange for the subsidies, the Eagles and Phillies each agreed to contribute a million dollars a year to a fund for children.[17]

Politicians and investors also promoted more gentrification. In the late twentieth century the process spread around the fringe of Center City and in other areas where attractive amenities, combined with concerted city efforts, helped establish a critical mass of upscale buyers. In the late 1960s and 1970s, priced out of Society Hill, young professionals, empty nesters, and investors bought up and remodeled the row houses below South Street in historic Southwark, renamed Queen Village. As property values rose in response, others moved west to the renamed Bella Vista, and to Fairmount, behind the Art Museum. Banks, which had shunned such areas for decades, now eagerly offered financing. Federal tax changes in 1981, offering accelerated depreciation for historic buildings, provided added incentives. Beginning in the 1980s, gentrification extended to Old City and in Powelton Village, near the University of Pennsylvania. A ten-year tax abatement program the city introduced in 1998 further encouraged the process. Farther afield, in Manayunk, investors converted abandoned factories to loft apartments that commanded substantial rents. After the year 2000 gentrification rapidly spread south of downtown into the Graduate Hospital area and in Passyunk below Bella Vista, farther west, surrounding University City, and north into Northern Liberties, Fishtown, and lower Kensington.[18]

Universities also became actively involved in neighborhood change, particularly after violent crimes around their campuses frightened students, parents, and staff. The University of Pennsylvania, for example, invested heavily in improving the area near its campus by sponsoring a business improvement district that cleaned up streets, installed new lighting, and hired guards to patrol the area. The university renovated abandoned houses and resold them, sometimes for less than the cost of the improvements, guaranteed mortgages

Gentrification, which has spread around the periphery of Center City, has sometimes embittered the people who have been displaced. This 2015 photograph shows a row of restored homes in the Fairmount section. (Author's collection.)

for its employees, developed key retail sites, and subsidized a neighborhood school (Penn-Alexander) that ranked among the best in the city. The combined impact was to accelerate gentrification in University City and generally make the area safer.[19]

In the new century Philadelphia ranked third in the nation in the size of its downtown population. The residents, mostly college educated, were certainly integral to making a new downtown into a self-sustaining process. By supporting restaurants, bars, clubs, and cultural venues, they made street life interesting, creating a cosmopolitan ambiance where office workers and tourists felt safe and business would want to locate. In 2016 almost four hundred restaurants offered outdoor seating, a mark of the vitality of downtown. The interactions between office employment, tourism, and downtown residents reinforced one another. In the new century greater Center City attracted a disproportionate share of the city's in-migrants, mostly a young, college-educated population.[20]

The detrimental effects of gentrification, however, first evident with Society Hill, remained all too apparent. The neighborhoods that gentrifiers moved into were established communities whose residents had dense social networks: people sat on their stoops and gossiped, visited nearby relatives, and supported local neighborhood associations, taverns, and clubs. Many were homeowners who maintained their properties, but their false façades and aluminum awnings represented a different aesthetic from the historic-preservationist values of the gentrifiers. Gentrification undermined those communities. As property values began to rise, so did tax assessments. In Queen Village taxes rose 300 percent from 1970 to 1978 alone. To renovate, landlords quickly evicted renters. The whole process made homeowners feel as though they were being pushed out of their own neighborhoods and caused considerable animosity. Some owners sold because they could not afford the increased property taxes, while others eagerly cashed out. Not until 2014 did the city make any effort to assist moderate-income long-term owners whose property taxes jumped sharply. The lower-income households that moved out tended to relocate to neighborhoods with poorer quality-of-life indicators. Gentrification also had a significant effect on the city's housing stock. Just between 2000 and 2015 the city lost one-fifth of its low-cost rental units and most of those losses came in gentrifying neighborhoods.[21]

To encourage private capital to invest in economic development, particularly in distressed neighborhoods, the city, state, and federal governments all offered a variety of tax incentives and subsidy programs. The combined effect of those programs was mixed. For example, a 2014 report concluded that one state subsidy initiative was an ineffective and costly way to stimulate jobs. Each new job created cost the city and state more than a hundred thousand dollars in tax subsidies. On the positive side, redevelopment of the Navy Yard property was a big success. The navy finally closed the yard in 1995, and, with financial support from the federal government, the city took over the twelve-hundred-acre site in 2000. Managed by PIDC, it attracted more than 145 firms and, in 2015, provided 11,500 jobs, more than were lost when the Navy Yard closed. In addition, Aker, a Norwegian company, built a new shipbuilding facility that employed more than 1,000 workers.[22] Despite those initiatives, Center City retailing continued to weaken. The Macy's chain took over the Strawbridge and Wanamaker stores, and, in 2006, closed Strawbridge's. The venerable Wanamaker's, Philadelphia's flagship department store, became a Macy's branch, occupying only a few floors of its grand emporium. Across Market Street, the Gallery, an indoor mall built in the 1970s and subsidized by urban renewal funds, failed to live up to its promise. Its anchor department store, Gimbels, went out of business in 1986 and was eventually replaced by a K-Mart. The Gallery closed entirely in 2014, with plans to reopen as an outlet center for high-end brands.

By the end of the century, Philadelphia had largely remade Center City as an attractive and competitive district for white-collar businesses. In 2015 almost three hundred thousand people worked in Greater Center City. Without the commuter rail tunnel, modern skyscrapers and hotels, new arts venues, gentrified neighborhoods, and a plethora of restaurants the city might have atrophied, but how much those projects helped its struggling population is moot.[23]

The New Philadelphians

In the half-century from 1965 to 2015, a new wave of immigration helped to revive the city. Philadelphia has always been a community of immigrants, with each new group enriching the city with its skills, culture, entrepreneurship, and strong work ethic. The recent immigrants' patterns of migration and adjustment are strikingly similar to the patterns of those who came a hundred years before: early pioneers clustered in neighborhoods that became the nucleus for a larger community; they sent for relatives, carved out niches in the economy, and established institutions to celebrate and maintain their identity.

People arrived from all over the world. In the 1960s and 1970s they came from Asia, especially from India, South Korea, the Philippines, Taiwan, Hong Kong, Vietnam, and Cambodia; in the 1980s and 1990s, from the Soviet Union and Eastern Bloc countries; after 1990, from the Caribbean islands and Central America, primarily Haiti, Jamaica, the Dominican Republic, and Mexico. The post-1990 wave also included refugees from war-torn countries in the Balkans, Africa, and the Middle East. Between 1990 and 2014, the foreign-born population doubled to 204,000, 13 percent of the total. In addition, there were more than 130,000 residents of Puerto Rican ancestry who, as citizens, are not considered foreign born. Philadelphia had the nation's second largest Puerto Rican community, and in the 2010s a new wave of migrants arrived from the island. The new migration had two profound effects: Philadelphia started growing again, with a net gain from 2000 to 2015 of 50,000 people, or 3.3 percent, and, in the 1990s non-Hispanic whites became a minority of the population. By 2015 their share had dropped to 35 percent, while non-Hispanic blacks accounted for 41 percent, all Hispanics 14 percent, and Asians 7 percent.[24]

Like the European immigrants who came a century earlier, these new settlers, with considerable sacrifice, carved out neighborhood and employment niches. Early pioneers among every group founded their own churches, beneficial and social service agencies, and cultural institutions. In most instances, neighborhoods grew from a small cluster around those facilities. When a wave of refugees arrived in a short time, resettlement agencies guided them to particular neighborhoods. The Hebrew Immigrant Aid Society assisted Holocaust survivors after World War II and later refugees from the Soviet Union. Established settlement houses, such as Catholic Social Services, and new agencies, such as Asian Americans United, Welcoming Center for New Pennsylvanians, and the Southeast Asian Mutual Assistance Associations Coalition, as well as churches and synagogues, reached out to help with housing, language classes, health care, and job placement.

In the early twenty-first century the newcomers concentrated in six areas. Although particular groups clustered together, there was considerable intermingling. With the exception of immigrants from Africa and Jamaica, newcomers avoided predominantly black neighborhoods and carved out communities in areas where the native-born white population was in decline. The largest Hispanic community lived in central North Philadelphia, between Germantown and Kensington Avenues. Puerto Ricans dominated, but the area included people from throughout Latin America, especially Dominicans. The city's most ethnically diverse neighborhoods lay just to the north, in East Oak Lane, Olney, Lawncrest, and Oxford Circle, where South Koreans dominated and shared space with East and Southeast Asians and Caribbean islanders. In the 1980s and 1990s, in the Far Northeast above Cottman Avenue and west of Roosevelt Boulevard, refugees from the former Soviet Union joined the large Jewish community that had settled there after World War II. By 2015, they were intermixed with a significant population from India.

South Philadelphia once again became a major immigrant destination, primarily east of Broad Street south of Washington Avenue, where, in the 1970s and 1980s, social service agencies settled Vietnamese and Cambodian refugees. In the 1990s, Mexicans also moved in as long-time Italian Americans moved out. Washington Avenue became a main shopping street of Asian and Mexican immigrants, who took over many of the stalls at the historic Italian Market centered at Ninth and Christian. University City attracted well-educated East Asians, South Asians, and West Africans, who worked at the universities and medical centers there. Elmwood and Eastwick in the far southwestern part of the city attracted people from Africa, particularly Liberia, and from the Caribbean and Vietnam.[25]

In Center City, the historic Chinatown district received an influx of Chinese immigrants as well as people from Vietnam (many of whom were ethnic Chinese), Indonesia, and Hong Kong. Holy Redeemer Chinese Catholic Church, opened at Tenth and Vine in 1941, became a vital anchor to the district. In the 1960s, plans for the Vine Street Expressway threatened to demolish the church and rip apart Chinatown. Out of the subsequent protests came

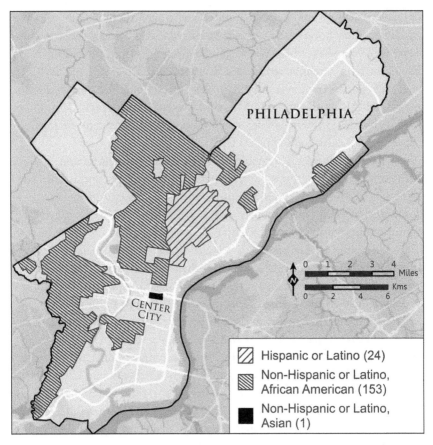

PHILADELPHIA

CENTER
CITY

0 1 2 3 4
Miles
Kms
0   2   4   6

Hispanic or Latino (24)

Non-Hispanic or Latino,
African American (153)

Non-Hispanic or Latino,
Asian (1)

This map shows the 2010 census tracts where a majority of the population identified as non-Hispanic African American, Hispanic, and non-Hispanic Asian. Asians did not constitute a majority outside of Chinatown; however, Olney, Oxford Circle, University City, and South Philadelphia (east of Broad, between Christian Street and Oregon Avenue) contained clusters of non-Hispanic Asians. (Prepared for The Pennsylvania History Association by Scott A. Drzyzga, Shippensburg University.)

the Philadelphia Chinatown Development Corporation, which helped protect the neighborhood from further displacement and sponsored several housing projects. Closed off from expansion to the south by the Gallery and the Convention Center, Chinatown spread north. In 2000 the community successfully fought plans for a baseball stadium at Twelfth and Vine. Most Chinese immigrants did not live in Chinatown, but, as before, it was their downtown.[26]

Immigrants were visible beyond their numbers and contributed disproportionately to the growth of the labor force. Many took low-wage jobs, but some became doctors, nurses, and other professionals. Among newer immigrants, South Asians and West Africans had the highest levels of education. Furthermore, the percentage of immigrants living in poverty was lower than that of the native-born population, and the percentage with a college degree was higher. Also, the percentage of immigrants who were self-employed was higher than that of the native born. With capital from their own savings and credit raised within the immigrant group, they established neighborhood grocery and convenience stores, restaurants, repair shops, and service businesses across the city. Their hard work helped revive and revitalize important shopping corridors, such as the Fifty-Second Street district.[27]

The new arrivals also faced resentment and endured discrimination in jobs, housing, and even the receipt of charity. Just as in the past, violence occasionally flared between new immigrants and long-established residents. For example, a 2009 investigation revealed widespread verbal and physical conflict among ethnic and racial groups in the public schools. City Hall made efforts to reach out to the immigrant communities and facilitate their integration into the life of the city with several programs to provide services in multiple languages. New immigrants have always held onto their culture, but now, because of globalization, including email, Skype, telephone service, and inexpensive air travel, recent immigrants maintain a transnational perspective, holding onto a strong affinity to their country of origin that has slowed their acculturation to American society.[28]

Boom and Bust

Beyond the gleam of new skyscrapers and upscale neighborhoods, Philadelphia continued to slide. Middle-class flight accelerated; from 1980 to 2010 the middle-class share of the city's population dropped from 55 to 42 percent. The population became poorer. By the turn of the century, median household income had fallen to 60 percent of the regional level, and 27 percent of the population (37 percent of children) survived on incomes below the poverty line, the highest share among the ten largest cities, but less than that of other Rust Belt cities such as Cleveland or Detroit. From 2000 to 2014 citywide median household income, adjusted for inflation, fell 10 percent, to $37,460.[29]

In the 1980s, the city witnessed an epidemic of crack cocaine abuse, a surge in homelessness, further deterioration of the schools, the AIDS epidemic, widespread property abandonment, rising crime rates, and even collapsing neighborhoods. The wave of homelessness resulted from a confluence of three main factors: gentrification and slum clearance eliminated much of the cheap housing around Center City, closure of state mental hospitals released mentally ill people onto the streets with little support, and deindustrialization eliminated jobs for low-skilled people. Homeless people gravitated to downtown, sleeping on steam vents, begging, and scaring commuters and tourists, leading businessmen to clamor for action. In the 1980s the city's response involved little more than offering blankets and hot drinks. Eventually, shelter facilities, social services, and aggressive policing reduced their visibility but not the problem. The CCD security force tried to keep homeless people away from tourists, but Love Park, Logan Circle, and Franklin Square were favored hangouts for some time. Eventually, churches and civic groups provided housing, social services, and food banks for thousands. Despite the Great Recession, which began in 2008, from 2008 to 2013 the number of homeless declined; still, in 2014, more than nine hundred people lived on the streets and twelve thousand used shelters for at least part of the year.[30]

Perhaps no factor better explains continued white out-migration than the dismal public schools—bad and growing steadily worse. An increasing proportion of children from poor and dysfunctional families drained resources and energy. (In 2014, one-third of families with children under eighteen had incomes below the poverty line.) Contentious relations with the teachers' union aggravated the problem. Philadelphia had a strong private and parochial school system, and as the minority population grew, whites in changing neighborhoods often pulled their children out of the public schools, weakening political support for public education and making those schools even more segregated than the city as a whole. In 2014, only 15 percent of public school students were non-Hispanic whites, attending mostly all-white schools. Critics and politicians blamed teachers, unions, parents, welfare, and new curricula for the low student performance; it was easier than blaming poverty or a lack of jobs.

In 2002, the state seized control of the schools and established the School Reform Commission to run them. The commission turned the most troubled schools over to a private corporation and expanded the number of charter schools, which were popular with middle-class residents; by 2013, 30 percent of students in publicly supported schools attended eighty charter schools. While charters may have benefited those enrolled, they drained the school budget further. Moreover, by drawing students from across the city, they weakened local schools, which are vital neighborhood anchors.

After the Great Recession of 2008, state cuts in school subsidies disproportionately hit Philadelphia; consequently, the commission fired thousands of teachers, counselors, librarians, and nurses and closed dozens of schools, reducing education to the most bare-bones level. Although the city increased its contribution to the school budget, total school spending per student in 2015, adjusted for inflation, was less than in 2007. In 2015 the district's sixth graders tested more than a full grade level below the national average in read-

In the twenty-first century, with financing from the federal government, most of the city's public housing projects were demolished and replaced with lower-density homes. This 2016 photograph shows the new Richard Allen Homes at Twelfth and Spring Garden Streets. (Author's collection.)

ing and math, with marked disparities between white and minority students. The best one might say is that other Rust Belt cities fared even worse because there were some positive indicators for Philadelphia; between 1997 and 2008 the high school graduate rate for entering freshmen rose from 50 to 64 percent, although rates for black and Hispanic males remained low.[31]

On the positive side, public housing experienced a turnaround. In the early 1990s, with almost a quarter of its inventory vacant, inefficient and corrupt management plagued the agency. In 1992, the federal government had to take over the PHA for two years to clean it up. During the next fifteen years, with federal grants, the housing authority replaced its oldest projects with new row houses and twins featuring small yards and off-street parking. The low-density, suburban appearance was a dramatic change from the barracks-like buildings and high-rise towers of older projects, although the new developments had fewer units than those they replaced. In some instances, the new public housing projects encouraged private capital to invest in adjacent areas. The PHA began to take a more comprehensive approach to neighborhood revival, integrating commercial space and social services with new housing, some of which could be sold at below market rates. The PHA also administered the federal Housing Choice Voucher Program (previously known as Section 8), which subsidized rent for low-income tenants in market-rate units. In 2005, sixteen thousand families took advantage of the voucher program, but the administration of George W. Bush reduced funding, and PHA closed its waiting list. Landlords had no obligation to participate, and the program did nothing to break down racial isolation. In 2015 PHA housed eighty thousand people in all of its programs.[32]

The lack of jobs, increased drug use, readily available guns, and a large population of young adult males created a toxic mix that led to a surge in street crime from the 1960s through the 1980s, demoralizing and undermining neighborhoods. But after peaking around 1990, crime rates fell sharply. Homicides dropped in half from 1990 to 2015, and Philadelphia's homicide rate no longer ranked among the top ten major cities. Better policing, a drop in the population of young adults, and perhaps just weariness with the mayhem account for the decline.[33] Nevertheless, hostility between the police and the black community inhibited investigations even though the vast majority of homicide victims continued to be African American—80 percent in 2014.

Incidents in the 1980s and 1990s only exacerbated antipathies of blacks toward the police. In addition to the MOVE debacle, in 1991 five policemen in the African American Tioga section pled guilty to planting drugs on innocent people and pocketing drug proceeds. Consequently, the court vacated almost three hundred convictions; an investigation in 2000 revealed continued police racial-profiling. Even more consequential was the national policy of aggressive policing to stem the more widespread use of drugs. Ever larger numbers of young black males were incarcerated for minor offences, such as failing to pay traffic fines, and for nonviolent drug crimes. In some instances, the criminal justice system looked like a debtors' prison. The resultant criminal records ruined the lives of black males and aggravated the siege mentality toward the police. Further, even as violent crime declined, the number of shootings by police increased. In 2012 police shot fifty-two suspects, twelve of whom died. It did not help that African Americans and Hispanics were significantly underrepresented on the police force. In 2007 Michael Nutter ran for mayor on a platform that called for police to "stop and frisk" supposedly suspect persons for drugs and weapons. As a 2010 lawsuit demonstrated, in practice the policy further reinforced racial profiling. Mayor James Kenney, who took office in 2016, promised to eliminate the policy.[34]

Deindustrialization, lack of jobs, the drug epidemic, and continued racial discrimination left the poorest neighborhoods looking like "ghost towns" of abandoned cars, vacant houses, trash-filled lots, and drug emporiums. In 1980, the city had thirty-seven thousand vacant housing units, although squatters occupied some of them. During the next two decades, the number of abandoned houses increased faster than the city could demolish them. By 2000, the number had increased to forty-seven thousand, and almost three hundred thousand people lived on a block with at least one abandoned house, enough to pull down the property values of the whole block. The improved economy of the 1990s enabled Rendell's administration, mostly using federal aid, to stabilize some neighborhoods by providing affordable housing, but it made little impact in the worst areas.[35]

Across the city residents resisted decline and fought for attention from City Hall. They organized nonprofit community development corporations (CDCs) to raise money for recreation venues, business development, affordable housing, social services, and jobs. Volunteers did much of the work at these bottom-up organizations. Although most centered on particular neighborhoods, some focused on specific populations or religious groups; by 2015 there were more than forty. Both the city and the state encouraged local businesses to support CDCs by providing tax credits. Local businessmen also established additional business improvement districts. By 2012, there were fourteen such districts, centered on commercial corridors, such as Aramingo, Germantown, and Passyunk Avenues, but the largest districts, in addition to Center City, served gentrified areas: University City, Old City, Mt. Airy, and Manayunk.[36]

John Street, mayor from 2000 to 2008, pledged to shift priorities from Center City to the neighborhoods and launched the bond-financed Neighborhood Transformation Initiative (NTI), which did make a difference, but the results were mixed. NTI towed thousands of abandoned cars, cleaned empty lots, and increased housing-code enforcement, but plans to demolish large numbers of abandoned houses proved costlier than anticipated. Demolition crews concentrated on areas with extensive blight, clearing parcels for developers. Homeowners found it easier to get improvement loans, and NTI facilitated the construction of sixteen thousand market-rate housing units and nine thousand units of affordable or public housing. But occupants of houses slated for demolition strenuously resisted the taking of their homes.[37]

Street's term coincided with a housing boom, so rising property and transfer taxes helped balance the budget. Although he tried to focus on distressed neighborhoods, as real estate prices escalated, private capital invested in expanding gentrification. During the housing boom, homeownership rates increased for African Americans and Hispanics, but unscrupulous banks and brokers often steered those buyers into subprime mortgages with higher rates that made the loans more vulnerable to default. In 2006, 58 percent of mortgage loans taken by African Americans were subprime, while for non-Hispanic whites the figure was 16 percent. During the Great Recession Philadelphia set up the Residential Mortgage Foreclosure Diversion Program to help homeowners in default save their properties.[38]

The Great Recession hit Philadelphia hard and recovery came slowly. For 2010 through 2013, the official unemployment rate exceeded 10 percent. By the summer of 2016 it had dropped to 7 percent, still 40 percent higher than the national average. The American Community Survey's broader definition indicated an overall unemployment rate of 11 percent, but 14.5 percent for Hispanics and 15.2 percent for African Americans. However unemployment was counted, economic opportunity for minorities remained grim. Health care and education led the economic recovery, but the job growth came mainly in low-wage positions. As of 2014, the region had not restored many of the high-wages jobs lost in the Recession.[39]

In 2007 Michael Nutter won election as the city's third African American mayor. Reelected in 2011, his term coincided with the Great Recession, during which tax revenues plummeted. In fiscal 2014 the city's revenue had still not returned to pre-recession levels. Recurrent financial crises forced Nutter to make substantial budget cuts and sharply reduce maintenance citywide. Although federal stimulus funds helped for a time, a deeply hostile Republican state administration sharply reduced aid to education. Between 2010 and 2015, the city increased its school allocation by almost four hundred million dollars, but it was not enough to cover state cuts. Nutter's austerity raised the city's bond rating to its highest level in decades. He introduced several initiatives to reduce crime and improve policing, but budget stringencies greatly limited his options.[40] Meanwhile, several federal and local programs attempted to address the impact of the Recession, coordinating social services, offering job training, and addressing a growing heroin epidemic. The city council in 2013 established a program to facilitate acquisition and transfer of thirty-two thousand vacant and abandoned properties to private sector investors.[41]

Despite the Recession, Greater Center City continued to attract investment and new residents. In 2008, Comcast, the nation's largest cable provider, opened its gleaming new headquarters at Seventeenth Street and Kennedy Boulevard. At 973 feet, it became the city's tallest building, and its Innovation and Technology Center, due to open next door in 2017, will rise 1,121 feet. In 2016, however, the Center City office occupancy rate still had not returned to its 2008 peak. The city invested in public spaces and amenities, enhancing the quality of life in many neighborhoods, but mostly around Center City. Franklin Square was redesigned as a family-friendly space in the historic district, with a carousel, a fountain, and a miniature golf course. A rebuilt Dilworth Park on the north side of City Hall quickly became a popular venue for down-

The mission of the Philadelphia Mural Arts Program, which began in 1985, has been to direct the energy of graffiti artists toward public projects. Now the nation's largest public arts program, it has sponsored hundreds of large murals throughout the city. *Philadelphia Muses* (shown here), which was painted in 1999, is located at Thirteenth and Locust Streets. (*Philadelphia Muses*, copyright © 1999 and 2013 City of Philadelphia Mural Arts Program/Meg Saligman. Photo by the author.)

town festivals. In 2014 Schuylkill Banks Boardwalk opened, a 2,000-foot walk that extends over the river on the east bank and connects with walking trails on either end. Plans were also under way for an elevated park on the abandoned Reading viaduct, similar to New York City's Highline.[42]

IN 2016 PHILADELPHIA was the nation's fifth largest city. Among the ten cities with more than one million people, Philadelphia did not look good. Its growth rate was weak, and it had the highest percentage of people living in poverty. But the comparison is deceptive. Seven of those ten cites are in the Sun Belt. A fairer comparison would be with other Rust Belt cities, such as Detroit, Baltimore, Cleveland, and St. Louis, all cities among the top ten in 1950. Measured against those cities, Philadelphia looked a lot better. It had weathered the transition to a postindustrial economy. It was attracting educated young adults and foreign immigrants, and its population was growing again. It made its business district more competitive for finance and insurance firms. It facilitated expansion of its higher education and medical sectors and invested in its cultural, recreational, and historic venues. Violent crime had fallen. Residential construction was the highest in a decade. Tourism was up, and the United Nations named Philadelphia a World Heritage City, the first in the United States.

But there remained another Philadelphia: more than four hundred thousand people survived on incomes below the poverty line. While the city became more diverse in the aggregate, it remained as segregated as ever at the neighborhood level. Gentrification continued to be controversial. The city had limited options to address community needs, particularly for its large impoverished population. It continued to face a hostile state legislature and suspicious suburbs and had to rely on private capital for almost all major initiatives. With a sluggish economy, unemployment remained stubbornly high. Business leadership seems preoccupied with Center City and reducing the taxes on business, but Philadelphia will be a successful community in the twenty-first century only if public and private capital invest in education, social welfare, and housing needs beyond the glamour of Center City.

APPENDIX

Tables

POPULATION OF PHILADELPHIA PROPER AND BUILT-UP AREA, 1683–1850		
	City proper	*Total urban area*
1693	2,044	
1720	4,659	4,883
1741	9,078	10,360
1767	15,870	22,814
1775	20,300	31,410
1782	28,414	38,798
1790	28,522	42,520
1800	41,220	67,811
1810	53,722	96,664
1820	63,802	119,325
1830	80,462	167,811
1840	93,665	228,871
1850	121,376	350,591

Sources: Gary B. Nash and Billy G. Smith, "The Population of Eighteenth-Century Philadelphia," *Pennsylvania Magazine of History and Biography* 99 (July 1975): 362–375; U.S. Bureau of the Census, Decennial Census, 1790–1850, available at https://www.census.gov/population/www/documentation/twps0027/twps0027.html.

POPULATION OF PHILADELPHIA, 1860–2015

	Population	Growth over preceding decade	Foreign born	% foreign born	Black*	% black	Hispanic†	% Hispanic	Asian	% Asian
1860	565,529	156,507	169,430	30.2	22,185	4.0				
1870	674,022	108,493	183,624	27.2	22,147	3.3				
1880	847,170	173,148	204,335	24.1	31,699	3.7				
1890	1,046,964	199,794	269,500	25.7	39,371	3.8				
1900	1,293,697	246,733	295,340	22.8	62,613	4.8				
1910	1,549,008	255,311	382,578	26.1	84,459	5.5				
1920	1,823,779	274,771	397,927	21.8	134,229	7.4				
1930	1,950,961	127,182	368,624	18.9	219,599	11.3				
1940	1,931,334	−19,627	290,325	15.0	250,880	13.0				
1950	2,071,605	140,271	232,587	11.2	376,041	18.2				
1960	2,002,512	−69,093	178,427	8.9	582,468	29.1				
1970	1,948,609	−53,903	129,109	6.5	653,747	33.5	45,798	2.4		
1980	1,688,210	−260,399	107,951	6.4	638,878	37.8	63,570	3.8	17,764	1.1
1990	1,585,577	−102,633	104,814	6.6	631,936	39.9	89,193	5.6	43,522	2.7
2000	1,517,550	−68,027	137,205	9.0	655,824	43.2	128,928	8.5	67,654	4.5
2010	1,528,338	10,788	192,095	12.6	661,839	43.3	187,611	12.3	96,405	6.3
2015	1,567,442	39,104	205,339	13.1	664,062	42.4	219,038	14.0	113,162	7.2

Sources: U.S. Bureau of the Census, Decennial Census, 1860–2010; U.S. Bureau of the Census, American Community Survey 5-Year Estimates, Selected Economic Characteristics, Philadelphia County, PA, 2011–2015; U.S. Bureau of the Census, 2015 American Community Survey 1-Year Estimate, 2015, Social Explorer, available at www.socialexplorer.com.

* Before 1960, figures are for all nonwhites.

† Hispanics include all races; not available before 1970.

POPULATION OF PHILADELPHIA METROPOLITAN AREA, 1930–2015

	Metropolitan area* (in millions)	Percentage of metropolitan area in Philadelphia
1930	3.137	62.2
1940	3.199	60.4
1950	3.671	56.4
1960	4.343	46.1
1970	4.824	40.4
1980	4.717	35.8
1990	4.857	32.7
2000	5.101	30.9
2010	5.260	29.0
2015	5.346	29.3

Sources: U.S. Bureau of the Census, Decennial Census, 1930–2010; U.S. Bureau of the Census, 2015 American Community Survey 1-Year Estimate, Social Explorer, available at www.socialexplorer.com.

* Includes Bucks, Chester, Delaware, Montgomery, and Philadelphia Counties in Pennsylvania and Burlington, Gloucester, and Camden Counties in New Jersey. In recent decades the U.S. Bureau of the Census has included Salem County, New Jersey, as part of the primary metropolitan area, but for consistency it is omitted here.

NOTES

Chapter 1

1. Gary Nash, *Quakers and Politics: Pennsylvania, 1681–1726* (Princeton, NJ: Princeton University Press, 1968); Joseph E. Illick, *Colonial Pennsylvania: A History* (New York: Scribner, 1976); Frederick B. Tolles, *Meeting House and Counting House* (Chapel Hill: University of North Carolina Press, 1948); Mary Maples Dunn and Richard Dunn, "The Founding, 1681–1701," in *Philadelphia: A 300-Year History,* ed. Russell F. Weigley, 1–32 (New York: W. W. Norton, 1982).

2. Jean R. Soderlund, *Lenape Country: Delaware Valley Society before William Penn* (Philadelphia: University of Pennsylvania Press, 2015).

3. John Reps, *Making of Urban America* (Princeton, NJ: Princeton University Press, 1965); Steven Conn, *Metropolitan Philadelphia: Living the Presence of the Past* (Philadelphia: University of Pennsylvania Press, 2006), 30–31; Elizabeth Milroy, *The Grid and the River: Philadelphia's Green Places, 1682–1876* (University Park: Pennsylvania State University Press, 2016), chap. 1; *The Encyclopedia of Greater Philadelphia,* s.v. "Elfreth's Alley," by Joanne Danifo, 2012, available at http://philadelphiaencyclopedia.org/.

4. Sam Bass Warner Jr., *The Private City: Philadelphia in Three Periods of its Growth* (Philadelphia: University of Pennsylvania Press, 1968), chap. 1; Edwin B. Bonner, "Village into Town, 1701–1746," and Theodore Thayer, "Town into City, 1746–1765," in Weigley, *Philadelphia,* 33–108; Thomas M. Doerflinger, *A Vigorous Spirit of Enterprise: Merchants and Economic Development in Revolutionary America* (Chapel Hill: University of North Carolina Press, 1986); John Bezis-Selfa, *Forging America: Ironworkers, Adventurers, and the Industrious Revolution* (Ithaca, NY: Cornell University Press, 2004); Sarah Fatherly, *Gentlewomen and Learned Ladies: Women and Elite Formation in Eighteenth-Century Philadelphia* (Bethlehem, PA: Lehigh University Press, 2008), chap. 1.

5. Carl Bridenbaugh, *Cities in Revolt: Urban Life in America, 1743–1776* (New York: Knopf, 1955); Judith Diamonstone, "The Government of Eighteenth Century Philadelphia," in *Town and Country: Essays on the Structure of Local Government in the American Colonies,* ed. Bruce C. Daniels (Middletown, CT: Wesleyan University Press, 1978); *Encyclopedia of Greater Philadelphia,* s.v. "Public Markets," by Helen Tangires, 2016.

6. Billy G. Smith, *The "Lower Sort": Philadelphia's Laboring People, 1750–1800* (Ithaca, NY: Cornell University Press, 1990), chap. 1.

7. Michal McMahon, "'Publick Service' versus 'Mans Properties': Dock Creek and the Origins of Urban Technology in Eighteenth-Century Philadelphia," in *Nature's Entrepôt: Philadelphia's Urban Sphere and Its Environmental Thresholds,* ed. Brian C. Black and Michael J. Chiarappa (Pittsburgh: University of Pittsburgh Press, 2012), 91–116.

8. Esmond Wright, *Franklin of Philadelphia* (Cambridge, MA: Belknap Press of Harvard University Press, 1986); Walter Isaacson, *Benjamin Franklin: An American Life* (New York: Simon and Schuster, 2003); *Encyclopedia of Greater Philadelphia,* s.v. "Anatomy and Anatomy Education," by Christopher Willoughby, 2015.

9. James T. Lemon, *Liberal Dreams and Nature's Limits: Great Cities of North America since 1600* (Toronto: Oxford University Press, 1996) chap. 3; Fatherly, *Gentlewomen,* chaps. 1–2; Milroy, *The Grid and the River,* chap. 4.

10. Elizabeth Sandwith Drinker, *The Diary of Elizabeth Drinker,* ed. Elaine Forman Crane (Boston: Northeastern University Press, 1994); Fatherly, *Gentlewomen,* chaps. 1–2; Karin Wulf, *Not All Wives: Women in Colonial Philadelphia* (Ithaca, NY: Cornell University Press, 2000), chap. 3.

11. Stuart M. Blumin, *The Emergence of the Middle Class: Social Experience in the American City, 1760–1900* (Cambridge: Cambridge University Press, 1989), chap. 2; Benjamin Franklin, *The Autobiography of Benjamin Franklin* (New York: Henry Holt and Company, 1916), available at https://www.gutenberg.org/files/20203/20203-h/20203-h.htm.

12. Wulf, *Not All Wives,* chaps. 3–4.

13. Simon P. Newman, *Embodied History: The Lives of the Poor in Early Philadelphia* (Philadelphia: University of Pennsylvania Press, 2003), 131; Smith, *"Lower Sort,"* chaps. 1, 3–4.

14. Clare A. Lyons, *Sex among the Rabble: An Intimate History of Gender and Power in the Age of Revolution, Philadelphia, 1730–1830* (Chapel Hill: University of North Carolina Press, 2006); Newman, *Embodied History,* chap. 1; Wulf, *Not All Wives,* chap. 3; Gary B. Nash and Billy G. Smith, "The Population of Eighteenth-Century Philadelphia," *Pennsylvania Magazine of History and Biography* 99 (July 1975): 362–375.

15. Gary B. Nash, *The Urban Crucible: Social Change, Political Consciousness, and the Origins of the American Revolution* (Cambridge, MA: Harvard University Press, 1979); John K. Alexander, *Render Them Submissive: Responses to Poverty in Philadelphia: 1760–1800* (Amherst: University of Massachusetts Press, 1980); Newman, *Embodied History,* chap. 1; Wulf, *Not All Wives,* chap. 5.

16. Gary B. Nash, *Forging Freedom: The Formation of Philadelphia's Black Community, 1720–1840* (Cambridge, MA: Harvard University Press, 1988), chap. 2; Gary B. Nash and Jean R. Soderlund, *Freedom by Degrees: Emancipation in Pennsylvania and its Aftermath* (New York: Oxford University Press, 1991), 17.

17. Peter Thompson, *Rum Punch and Revolution: Taverngoing and Public Life in Eighteenth-Century Philadelphia* (Philadelphia: University of Pennsylvania Press, 1999); Lyons, *Sex among the Rabble,* chaps. 2, 4, 5; Wulf, *Not All Wives,* chap. 3; *Encyclopedia of Greater Philadelphia,* s.v. "Coffeehouses," by Michelle Craig McDonald, 2016.

18. Carol Faulkner, *Lucretia Mott's Heresy: Abolition and Women's Rights in Nineteenth-Century America* (Philadelphia: University of Pennsylvania Press, 2011), 10.

19. Nash and Soderlund, *Freedom by Degrees,* chaps. 4–5; Nash, *Forging Freedom;* Newman, *Embodied History,* chap. 4; *Encyclopedia of Greater Philadelphia,* s.v. "Slavery and the Slave Trade," by James Gigantino, 2012.

20. Harry M. Tinkcom, "The Revolutionary City," in Weigley, *Philadelphia,* 109–154; Warner, *Private City,* chap 2; Simon P. Newman, *Parades and Politics of the Street: Festive*

Culture in the Early American Republic (Philadelphia: University of Pennsylvania Press, 1997), chap. 1.

21. Ronald Schultz, *Republic of Labor: Philadelphia Artisans and the Politics of Class, 1720–1830* (New York: Oxford University Press, 1993), chaps. 1–2.

22. Bruce Laurie, *Working People of Philadelphia, 1800–1850* (Philadelphia: Temple University Press, 1980), 1–3.

23. Newman, *Parades and Politics*, 40–42; Richard G. Miller, "The Federal City, 1783–1800," in Weigley, *Philadelphia*, 155–207; Smith, *"Lower Sort,"* chap. 3; Schultz, *Republic of Labor*, chap. 3.

24. J. Thomas Scharf and Thompson Westcott, *History of Philadelphia, 1609–1884* (Philadelphia: L. H. Evarts, 1884), vol. 1, 454–455.

25. Newman, *Parades and Politics*.

26. Smith, *"Lower Sort,"* 8; Miller, "The Federal City," 180-188; *Encyclopedia of Greater Philadelphia*, s.v. "Yellow Fever," by Simon Finger, 2011; Thomas Apel, "The Rise and Fall of Yellow Fever in Philadelphia, 1793–1805," in Black and Chiarappa, *Nature's Entrepôt*, 55–72.

Chapter 2

1. Diane Lindstrom, *Economic Development in the Philadelphia Region: 1810–1850* (New York: Columbia University Press, 1978).

2. Edward J. Gibbons, "The Building of the Schuylkill Navigation System, 1815–1828," *Pennsylvania History* 57 (January 1990): 13–43; Edgar P. Richardson, "The Athens of America: 1800–1825," 208–257, Nicholas B. Wainwright, "The Age of Nicholas Biddle: 1825–1841," 259–306, and Elizabeth M. Geffen, "Industrial Development and Social Crisis: 1841–1854," 307–362, in Weigley, *Philadelphia*; *Encyclopedia of Greater Philadelphia*, s.v. "Coal," by Thomas Mackaman, 2016.

3. Geffen, "Industrial Development"; Russell F. Weigley, "The Border City in Civil War, 1854–1865," in Weigley, *Philadelphia*, 368; Jeffrey P. Roberts, "Railroads and the Downtown: Philadelphia, 1830–1900," in *The Divided Metropolis: Social and Spatial Dimensions of Philadelphia*, ed. William M. Cutler and Howard Gillette (Westport, CT: Greenwood Press, 1980), chap. 2.

4. Lindstrom, *Economic Development*, chap. 6; Warner, *Private City*, chaps. 3–4.

5. Eugene S. Ferguson, *Oliver Evans, Inventive Genius of the American Industrial Revolution* (Greenville, DE: Hagley Museum, 1980).

6. John K. Brown, *The Baldwin Locomotive Works, 1831–1915* (Baltimore: Johns Hopkins University Press, 1995), chap. 1.

7. *Encyclopedia of Greater Philadelphia*, s.v. "Chemical Industry," by John Kenly Smith Jr., 2016;Thomas R. Heinrich, *Ships for the Seven Seas: Philadelphia Shipbuilding in the Age of Industrial Capitalism* (Baltimore: Johns Hopkins University Press, 1997).

8. *Encyclopedia of Greater Philadelphia*, s.v. "City of Medicine," by Steven J. Peitzman, 2016, s.v. "Woman's Medical College of Pennsylvania," by Melissa M. Mandell, 2016, and Willoughby, "Anatomy and Anatomy Education." Both colleges are now part of Drexel University College of Medicine.

9. Bruce Sinclair, *Philadelphia's Philosopher Mechanics: A History of the Franklin Institute, 1824–1865* (Baltimore: Johns Hopkins University Press 1974); Domenic Vitiello, *Engineering Philadelphia: The Sellers Family and the Industrial Metropolis* (Ithaca, NY: Cornell University Press, 2013), chap. 1.

10. Wainwright, "Age of Nicholas Biddle," 259–306; Warner, *Private City*, 54.

11. Warner, *Private City*, chap. 3; Weigley, "Border City," 372–383.

12. Warner, *Private City*, 54; Roberts, "Railroads and the Downtown."

13. Warner, *Private City*, chap. 3; Alan N. Burstein, "Immigrants and Residential Mobility: The Irish and Germans in Philadelphia, 1850–1880, in *Philadelphia: Work, Space, Family, and Group Experience in the Nineteenth Century, Essays toward an Interdisciplinary History of the City*, ed. Theodore Hershberg (New York: Oxford University Press, 1981), chap. 5.

14. Deborah C. Andrews, "Bank Buildings in Nineteenth-Century Philadelphia," in Cutler and Gillette, *Divided Metropolis*, chap. 3; Blumin, *Emergence of the Middle Class*, chap. 3; George Rogers Taylor, "'Philadelphia in Slices' by George G. Foster," *Pennsylvania Magazine of History and Biography* 93 (January 1969): 28–30, 55–60.

15. E. Digby Baltzell, *Philadelphia Gentlemen: The Making of a National Upper Class* (Glencoe, IL: Free Press, 1958); Milroy, *The Grid and the River*, 306–307.

16. Warner, *Private City*, chap. 6; Blumin, *Emergence of the Middle Class*, chap 5.

17. Theodore Hershberg, Harold E. Cox, Dale B. Light Jr., and Richard R. Greenfield, "The 'Journey to Work': An Empirical Investigation of Work, Residence and Transportation, Philadelphia, 1850 and 1880," in Hershberg, *Philadelphia*, chap. 4; Donna J. Rilling, *Making Houses, Crafting Capitalism: Builders in Philadelphia, 1790–1850* (Philadelphia: University of Pennsylvania Press, 2001), chaps. 1–2.

18. Laurie, *Working People*, chap. 1; Bruce Laurie and Mark Schmitz, "Manufacturing and Productivity: The Making of an Industrial Base, Philadelphia, 1850–1880," in Hershberg, *Philadelphia*, chap. 2; Warner, *Private City*, chap. 4.

19. Laurie, *Working People*, chap. 1; Cynthia J. Shelton, *The Mills of Manayunk: Industrialization and Social Conflict in the Philadelphia Region, 1787–1837* (Baltimore: Johns Hopkins University Press, 1986).

20. Jerome P. Bjelopera, *City of Clerks: Office and Sales Workers in Philadelphia, 1870–1920* (Urbana: University of Illinois Press, 2005), chap. 1; Blumin, *Emergence of the Middle Class*, chap. 5; Dennis Clark, *The Irish in Philadelphia: Ten Generations of Urban Experience* (Philadelphia: Temple University Press, 1973), chap. 3; Warner, *Private City*, chap. 4; Sam Alewitz, *"Filthy Dirty": A Social History of Unsanitary Philadelphia in the Late Nineteenth Century* (New York: Garland, 1989), 13.

21. Laurie, *Working People*, chap. 3; Geffen, "Industrial Development"; Clark, *Irish in Philadelphia*, chap. 6; Dennis Clark, "'Ramcat' and Rittenhouse Square: Related Communities," in Cutler and Gillette, *Divided Metropolis*, chap. 5; Taylor, "'Philadelphia in Slices,'" 34–38. George G. Foster is best known for his vignettes on New York; see *New-York in Slices* (1849?) and *New-York by Gas-Light* (1850).

22. Susan G. Davis, *Parades and Power: Street Theatre in Nineteenth-Century Philadelphia* (Berkeley: University of California Press, 1986); Schultz, *Republic of Labor*, chaps. 5–7; Shelton, *Mills of Manayunk*, chaps. 6–8; Philip Scranton, *Proprietary Capitalism: The Textile Manufacture at Philadelphia, 1800–1885* (Cambridge, MA: Cambridge University Press, 1983), chap. 5; Laurie, *Working People*, chaps. 5–9.

23. Nash, *Forging Freedom*, chap. 6; W. E. B. Du Bois, *The Philadelphia Negro* (Philadelphia: University of Pennsylvania Press,1899), chap. 4; Warner, *Private City*, chap. 7; Beverly C. Tomek, *Pennsylvania Hall: A 'Legal Lynching' in the Shadow of the Liberty Bell* (New York: Oxford University Press, 2014), chaps. 3–4.

24. Theodore Hershberg, "Free Blacks in Antebellum Philadelphia: A Study of Ex-slaves, Freeborn, and Socioeconomic Decline," in Hershberg, *Philadelphia*, chap. 11; Nash, *Forging Freedom*, chap. 8; Nick Salvatore, *We All Got History: The Memory Book of Amos Webber* (New York: Vintage, 1996), chap. 3.

25. Hershberg, "Free Blacks," 378–380.

26. *Encyclopedia of Greater Philadelphia,* s.v. "Vigilance Committees," by Beverly C. Tomek, 2015.

27. Clark, *Irish in Philadelphia;* chaps. 1–2; Michael Feldberg, *Philadelphia Riots of 1844: A Study in Ethnic Conflict* (Westport, CT: Greenwood Press, 1975), chap. 2.

28. Clark, *Irish in Philadelphia,* chap. 3; Bruce Laurie, Theodore Hershberg, and George Alter, "Immigrants and Industry: The Philadelphia Experience, 1850–1880," in Hershberg, *Philadelphia,* chap. 3; Burstein, "Immigrants and Residential Mobility"; Scranton, *Proprietary Capitalism,* chaps. 6–7; Warner, *Private City,* chap. 3.

29. Feldberg, *Philadelphia Riots,* chaps. 3–4.

30. Ibid.; Amanda Beyer-Purvis, "The Philadelphia Bible Riots of 1844: Contest over the Rights of Citizens," *Pennsylvania History* 83 (Summer 2016): 366–393.

31. Feldberg, *Philadelphia Riots,* chaps. 5–9.

32. Newman, *Embodied History;* David Rothman, *Discovery of the Asylum: Social Order and Disorder in the New Republic* (Boston: Little, Brown: 1971); Priscilla Ferguson Clement, *Welfare and the Poor in the Nineteenth-Century City: Philadelphia, 1800–1854* (Rutherford, NJ: Farleigh Dickinson University Press, 1985); Benjamin J. Klebaner, "The Home Relief Controversy in Philadelphia, 1782–1861," *Pennsylvania Magazine of History and Biography* 78 (October 1954): 413–423.

33. J. Matthew Gallman, *Receiving Erin's Children: Philadelphia, Liverpool, and the Irish Famine Migration, 1845–1855* (Chapel Hill: University of North Carolina Press, 2000); Eudice Glassberg, "Philadelphians in Need: Client Experiences in Two Philadelphia Benevolent Societies, 1830–1880" (D.S.W. diss., University of Pennsylvania, 1979).

34. Apel, "The Rise and Fall of Yellow Fever in Philadelphia," 70-72; Nelson Blake, *Water for the Cities: A History of the Urban Water Supply Problem in the United States* (Syracuse, NY: Syracuse University Press, 1956), chaps. 1–5; Smith, *City Water,* chaps. 2–3; Milroy, *The Grid and the River,* chap. 8; *Encyclopedia of Greater Philadelphia,* s.v. "Cholera," by John B. Osborne, 2010.

35. Smith, *City Water,* chap. 4; Taylor, "'Philadelphia in Slices,'" 65–68; David Schuyler, *The New Urban Landscape: The Redefinition of City Form in Nineteenth-Century America* (Baltimore; Johns Hopkins University Press, 1986), 102–108; Robert P. Armstrong, "Green Space in the Gritty City: The Planning and Development of Philadelphia's Park System, 1854–1929" (Ph.D. diss., Lehigh University, 2012), chap. 1; Milroy, *The Grid and the River,* chap. 10.

36. Warner, *Private City,* 111–123; Nash, *Forging Freedom,* chap. 6; *Encyclopedia of Greater Philadelphia,* s.v. "Public Education: The School District of Philadelphia," by William W. Cutler III, 2012.

37. Richardson, "Athens of America," 208–257.

38. Wainwright, "Age of Nicholas Biddle"; Geffen, "Industrial Development," 327–335; Baltzell, *Philadelphia Gentlemen,* chap. 5; E. Digby Baltzell, *The Protestant Establishment: Aristocracy and Caste in America* (New York: Vintage, 1966).

39. Warner, *Private City,* 102–111; Weigley, "Border City," 373.

40. Howard Gillette Jr., "The Emergence of the Modern Metropolis: Philadelphia in the Age of Consolidation," in Cutler and Gillette, *Divided Metropolis,* chap 1.

41. Gillette, "Emergence of the Modern Metropolis."

42. Faulkner, *Lucretia Mott,* chap. 5; Tomek, *Pennsylvania Hall.*

43. Weigley, "Border City," 363–416; Russell F. Weigley, "'A Peaceful City': Public Order in Philadelphia from Consolidation through the Civil War," in *The Peoples of Philadelphia: A History of Ethnic Groups and Lower-Class Life, 1790–1940,* ed. Allen F. Davis and Mark H. Haller (Philadelphia: Temple University Press, 1973), chap. 8; Heinrich, *Ships for the Seven*

Seas; James Gallman, "Preserving the Peace: Order and Disorder in Civil War Philadelphia," *Pennsylvania History* 55 (October 1988): 201–215; Du Bois, *Philadelphia Negro*, 38–39; *Encyclopedia of Greater Philadelphia*, s.v. "Arsenals," by Jean-Pierre Beugoms, 2015.

Chapter 3

1. Philip Scranton and Walter Licht, introduction to *Work Sights: Industrial Philadelphia, 1890–1960* (Philadelphia: Temple University Press, 1986).

2. Philip Scranton, *Figured Tapestry: Production, Markets, and Power in Philadelphia Textiles, 1885–1941* (Cambridge: Cambridge University Press, 1989); U.S. Bureau of the Census, *Thirteenth Census, 1910, Manufactures*, vols. 8, 9 (Washington, DC: Government Printing Office, 1912, 1913).

3. Brown, *Baldwin Locomotive Works*, chaps. 4–7; Vitiello, *Engineering Philadelphia*, chap. 3.

4. Heinrich, *Ships for the Seven Seas*; Vitiello, *Engineering Philadelphia*, chap. 3; Caroline Golab, *Immigrant Destinations* (Philadelphia: Temple University Press, 1977), chap. 6; Scranton and Licht, *Work Sights*, 147–270.

5. Scranton and Licht, *Work Sights*, 79–84.

6. John Henry Hepp IV, *The Middle-Class City: Transforming Space and Time in Philadelphia, 1876–1926* (Philadelphia: University of Pennsylvania Press, 2003), chap. 1; Dorothy Gondos Beer, "The Centennial City: 1865–1876," in Weigley, *Philadelphia*, 417–470; Andrews, "Bank Buildings in Nineteenth-Century Philadelphia."

7. Michael P. McCarthy, "Traditions in Conflict: The Philadelphia City Hall Site Controversy," *Pennsylvania History* 57 (October 1990): 301–317; Hepp, *Middle-Class City*, chap. 2; Tangires, "Public Markets."

8. Hepp, *Middle-Class City*, chap. 3; William Leach, *Land of Desire: Merchants, Power, and the Rise of a New American Culture* (New York: Pantheon, 1993); Gunther Barth, *City People* (New York: Oxford University Press, 1980), chap. 4.

9. Brian Alnutt, "African American Amusement and Recreation in Philadelphia, 1876–1926" (Ph.D. diss. Lehigh University, 2003); *Encyclopedia of Greater Philadelphia*, s.v. "Tenderloin," by Annie Anderson, 2016.

10. Hepp, *Middle-Class City*, chap. 1.

11. Armstrong, "Green Space in the Gritty City," chaps. 2–5; Milroy, *The Grid and the River*, chaps. 11–12; Adam Levine, "The Grid versus Nature," in Black and Chiarappa, *Nature's Entrepôt*, chap. 7.

12. Warner, *Private City*, chap. 10; William W. Cutler III, "The Persistent Dualism: Centralization and Decentralization in Philadelphia, 1854–1975," in Cutler and Gillette, *Divided Metropolis*, chap. 10.

13. Walter Licht, *Getting Work: Philadelphia, 1840–1950* (Cambridge, MA: Harvard University Press, 1992), chaps. 2, 3, 7; Michael R. Haines, "Poverty, Economic Stress, and the Family in a Late Nineteenth-Century American City: Whites in Philadelphia, 1880," and Claudia Goldin, "Family Strategies and the Family Economy in the Late Nineteenth Century: The Role of Secondary Workers," in Hershberg, *Philadelphia*, chaps. 7, 8.

14. Scranton, *Proprietary Capitalism*, chap. 10; Scranton, *Figured Tapestry*, chap. 5; Susan Levine, *Labor's True Woman: Carpet Weavers, Industrialization, and Labor Reform in the Gilded Age* (Philadelphia: Temple University Press, 1984), chap. 2; Peter Cole, *Wobblies on the Waterfront: Interracial Unionism in Progressive-Era Philadelphia* (Urbana: University of Illinois Press, 2007), chap. 2.

15. Cole, *Wobblies on the Waterfront*, 36–37; Daniel Sidorick, "The 'Girl Army': Phila-

delphia Shirtwaist Strike of 1909–1910," *Pennsylvania History* 71 (Summer 2004): 323–369; Brown, *Baldwin Locomotive Works,* 217–219; Henrich, *Ships for the Seven Seas.*

16. Scranton, *Figured Tapestry,* chaps. 2, 4; *Encyclopedia of Greater Philadelphia,* s.v. "General Strike of 1910," by Julianne Kornacki, 2015.

17. Licht, *Getting Work,* chaps. 5–6.

18. U.S. Bureau of the Census, *Thirteenth Census, 1910, Population,* vol. 1 (Washington, DC: Government Printing Office, 1913), 989–991.

19. Burstein, "Immigrants and Residential Mobility"; Theodore Hershberg, Alan N. Burstein, Eugene P. Ericksen, Stephanie Greenberg, and William L. Yancey, "A Tale of Three Cities: Blacks, Immigrants, and Opportunity in Philadelphia, 1850–1880, 1930, 1970," in Hershberg, *Philadelphia,* chap. 14; Ayumi Takenaka and Mary Johnson Osirim, "Philadelphia's Immigrant Communities in Historical Perspective," in *Global Philadelphia: Immigrant Communities Old and New,* ed. Ayumi Takenaka and Mary Johnson Osirim (Philadelphia: Temple University Press, 2010), chap. 1; Washington Avenue Immigration Station Historical Marker, http://explorepahistory.com/hmarker.php?markerId=1-A-3D7.

20. Richard N. Juliani, *Building Little Italy: Philadelphia's Italians before Mass Migration* (State College: Pennsylvania State University Press, 1998); Stefano Luconi, *From Paesani to White Ethnics: The Italian Experience in Philadelphia* (Albany: State University of New York Press, 2001), chaps. 2–3; Richard A. Varbero, "Workers in City and Country: The South Italian Experience in Philadelphia, 1900–1950," in *Italian Americans: The Search for a Useable Past,* ed. Richard N. Juliani and Philip V. Cannistraro (New York: American Italian Historical Association, 1989), chap. 5; Golab, *Immigrant Destinations,* pt. 1, appendixes; *Encyclopedia of Greater Philadelphia,* s.v. "Italian Market," by Helen Tangires, 2011; Kathryn E. Wilson, *Ethnic Renewal in Philadelphia's Chinatown: Space, Place, and Struggle* (Philadelphia: Temple University Press, 2015), chap. 1.

21. Golab, *Immigrant Destinations,* chap. 5–6, appendixes; Juliani, *Building Little Italy.*

22. Philip S. Foner, "The Battle to End Discrimination against Negroes on Philadelphia Streetcars (Part I): Background and Beginnings of the Battle," and "The Battle to End Discrimination against Negroes on Philadelphia Streetcars (Part II): The Victory," *Pennsylvania History* 40 (July and October 1973): 261–292, 354–379; Harry C. Silcox, "Nineteenth Century Philadelphia Black Militant: Octavius V. Catto," *Pennsylvania History* 44 (January 1977): 53–76.

23. Licht, *Getting Work,* chaps. 2, 7; W.E.B. Du Bois, *The Philadelphia Negro: A Social Study* (1899; reprint, Philadelphia: University of Pennsylvania Press, 1996); James Wolfinger, *Philadelphia Divided: Race and Politics in the City of Brotherly Love* (Chapel Hill: University of North Carolina Press, 2007), chap. 1; Warner, *Private City,* 183–185; Cole, *Wobblies on the Waterfront.*

24. Vincent Franklin, *Education of Black Philadelphia: The Social and Educational History of a Minority Community, 1900–1950* (Philadelphia: University of Pennsylvania Press, 1979); Du Bois, *Philadelphia Negro*; Alnutt, "African American Amusement."

25. John F. Sutherland, "City of Homes: Philadelphia Slums and Reformers, 1880–1918" (Ph.D. diss., Temple University, 1973), 225–232; V. P. Franklin, "The Philadelphia Race Riot of 1918," *Pennsylvania Magazine of History and Biography* 99 (July 1975): 336–350; Wolfinger, *Philadelphia Divided,* chap. 1; Frederic Miller, "The Black Migration to Philadelphia: A 1924 Profile," *Pennsylvania Magazine of History and Biography* 108 (July 1984): 315–350.

26. Bjelopera, *City of Clerks,* introduction, chaps. 1–2.

27. Roger Miller and Joseph Siry, "The Emerging Suburb: West Philadelphia, 1850–1880," *Pennsylvania History* 46 (April 1980): 99–146; Hepp, *Middle-Class City,* chap. 7, quotation on 193; Margaret Marsh, "The Impact of the Market Street 'El' on Northern West Philadelphia,

1900–1930: Environmental Change and Social Transformation, 1900–1930," in Cutler and Gillette, *Divided Metropolis,* chap. 7; Warner, *Private City,* chap. 8; Hershberg et al., "A Tale of Three Cities."

28. Meredith Savery, "Instability and Uniformity: Residential Patterns in Two Philadelphia Neighborhoods, 1880–1970," in Cutler and Gillette, *Divided Metropolis,* chap. 8.

29. David R. Contosta, *Suburb in the City: Chestnut Hill, Philadelphia, 1850–1990* (Columbus: Ohio State University Press, 1992); Margaret Marsh, *Suburban Lives* (New Brunswick, NJ: Rutgers University Press, 1990), chap. 4.

30. Lincoln Steffens, *The Shame of the Cities* (1904; reprint, New York: Hill and Wang, 1957), 134–161; John T. Salter, "Party Organization in Philadelphia: The Ward Committeeman," *American Political Science Review* 27 (August 1933): 618–627; Peter McCaffery, *When Bosses Ruled Philadelphia: The Emergence of the Republican Machine, 1867–1933* (University Park: Pennsylvania State University Press, 1993); quotation from Armstrong, "Green Space in the Gritty City," 140.

31. Ershkowitz, "Philadelphia Gas Works"; Milroy, *The Grid and the River,* 333–334.

32. Sutherland, "City of Homes," chap. 5; William H. Issel, "Modernization in Philadelphia School Reform, 1882–1905," *Pennsylvania Magazine of History and Biography* 94 (July 1970): 358–383; Cutler, "Public Education."

33. Beer, "Centennial City."

34. James E. Higgins, "Keystone of an Epidemic: Pennsylvania's Urban Experience during the 1918–1920 Influenza Epidemic" (Ph.D. diss., Lehigh University, 2009), chap. 3; Armstrong, "Green Space in the Gritty City," chap. 4.

35. Arthur P. Dudden, "The City Embraces 'Normalcy,' 1919–1929," in Weigley, *Philadelphia,* 592–596. In 2012 the Barnes collection relocated to a new building along the Parkway.

36. Hepp, *Middle-Class City,* chap. 7; Bjelopera, *City of Clerks,* chap. 4; Silas Chamberlin, "On the Trail: A History of American Hiking" (Ph.D. diss., Lehigh University, 2014); Armstrong, "Green Space in the Gritty City," chaps. 2–4.

37. Bruce Kuklick, *To Every Thing a Season: Shibe Park and Urban Philadelphia* (Princeton, NJ: Princeton University Press, 1991); Michael P. McCarthy, "The Unprogressive City: Philadelphia and Urban Stereotypes at the Turn of the Century," *Pennsylvania History* 54 (October 1987): 264–281.

38. Lloyd M. Abernathy, "Progressivism, 1905–1919," in Weigley, *Philadelphia,* 524–565; *Encyclopedia of Greater Philadelphia,* s.v. "World War I," by Jacob Downs, 2014.

39. Scranton, *Figured Tapestry,* chaps. 5–6; Henrich, *Ships for the Seven Seas*; Cole, *Wobblies on the Waterfront,* chap. 8.

40. Charles Abrams, *Home Ownership for the Poor: A Program for Philadelphia* (New York: Praeger, 1970), 89; Muller, "Urban Home Ownership"; Licht, *Getting Work,* chap. 7; Scranton, *Figured Tapestry,* chap. 6. By 1930, 55 percent of families had a radio and half of all families owned a home.

41. Sadie Tanner Mossell, "The Standard of Living among One Hundred Negro Migrant Families in Philadelphia," *Annals of the American Academy of Political and Social Science* 98 (November 1921): 173–218; Abrams, *Home Ownership*; Miller, "Black Migration to Philadelphia."

42. *Encyclopedia of Greater Philadelphia,* s.v. "Prohibition."

43. Daniel Amsterdam, *Roaring Metropolis: Businessmen's Campaign for a Civic Welfare State* (Philadelphia, University of Pennsylvania Press, 2016); Conn, *Metropolitan Philadelphia,* 80.

Chapter 4

1. U.S. Bureau of the Census, *Fifteenth Census, 1930, Unemployment,* vol. 2 (Washington, DC: Government Printing Office, 1932); State Emergency Relief Board, *Unemployment Relief in Pennsylvania: Sept. 1, 1932–Dec. 31, 1935,* Third Annual Report (Harrisburg, PA: State

Emergency Relief Administration, 1936); R. Daniel Wadhwani, "Soothing the People's Panic: The Banking Crisis of the 1930s in Philadelphia," *Pennsylvania Legacies* 11 (May 2011): 24–31. For a more detailed summary of the Depression, see *Encyclopedia of Greater Philadelphia,* s.v. "Great Depression," by Roger D. Simon, 2013.

2. John F. Bauman, "The City, the Depression, and Relief: The Philadelphia Experience, 1929–1939" (Ph.D. diss., Rutgers University, 1969); Margaret Tinkcom, "Depression and War, 1929–1946," in Weigley, *Philadelphia,* 601–648; Ewan Clague and Webster Powell, *Ten Thousand Out of Work* (Philadelphia: University of Pennsylvania Press, 1933).

3. Tinkcom, "Depression and War," 606–619; Bonnie R. Fox, "Unemployment Relief in Philadelphia, 1930–1932: A Study in the Depression's Impact on Voluntarism," *Pennsylvania Magazine of History and Biography* 93 (January 1969): 86–108.

4. James Wolfinger, *Philadelphia Divided: Race and Politics in the City of Brotherly Love* (Chapel Hill: University of North Carolina Press, 2007), 48; Francis Ryan, *AFSCME's Philadelphia Story: Municipal Workers and Union Power in the Twentieth Century* (Philadelphia: Temple University Press, 2011), chaps. 1–2; Luconi, *From Paesani to White Ethnics,* chap. 4.

5. John F. Bauman, Norman P. Hummon, and Edward K. Muller, "Public Housing, Isolation, and the Urban Underclass: Philadelphia's Richard Allen Homes, 1941–1965," *Journal of Urban History* 17 (May 1991): 264–292; John F. Bauman, *Public Housing, Race, and Renewal: Urban Planning in Philadelphia, 1920–1974* (Philadelphia: Temple University Press, 1987); Wolfinger, *Philadelphia Divided,* chaps. 3–4.

6. Amy Hillier, "Who Received Loans? Home Owners' Loan Corporation Lending and Discrimination in Philadelphia in the 1930s," *Journal of Planning History* 2 (2003): 3–24.

7. Elizabeth Fones-Wolf, "Industrial Unionism and Labor Movement Culture in Depression-Era Philadelphia," *Pennsylvania Magazine of History and Biography* 109 (1985): 3–26; Wolfinger, *Philadelphia Divided,* chap. 2; Ryan, *AFSCME's Philadelphia Story,* chap. 2.

8. John L. Shover, "The Emergence of a Two-Party System in Republican Philadelphia, 1924–1936," *Journal of American History* 60 (March 1974): 985–1002; Wolfinger, *Philadelphia Divided,* 49–53.

9. Alan Frazier, "Philadelphia: City of Brotherly Loot," *American Mercury,* July 1939, 275–282.

10. Tinkcom, "Depression and War," 638–645; Wolfinger, *Philadelphia Divided,* chap. 4; *Encyclopedia of Greater Philadelphia,* s.v. "World War II," by Herbert Ershkowitz, 2011.

11. Allan Winkler, "The Philadelphia Transit Strike of 1944," *Journal of American History* 59 (June 1972): 73–89; James Wolfinger, *Philadelphia Divided,* chaps. 5–6; James Wolfinger, *Running the Rails: Capital and Labor in Philadelphia's Transit Industry* (Ithaca, NY: Cornell University Press, 2016), chap. 5. The Philadelphia Rapid Transit Company was reorganized as the Philadelphia Transportation Company during bankruptcy proceedings in the 1930s. It was generally known as the PTC.

12. Ryan, *AFSCME's Philadelphia Story,* 103.

13. Marquis W. Childs and John Coburn Turner, "The Real Philadelphia Story," *Forum and Century,* June 1940, 289–294; Ryan, *AFSCME's Philadelphia Story,* 109–110; Jeanne R. Lowe, *Cities in a Race with Time: Progress and Poverty in America's Renewing Cities* (New York: Random House, 1967), chap. 8. For the national context, see Jon C. Teaford, *The Rough Road to Renaissance: Urban Revitalization in American, 1940–1985* (Baltimore: Johns Hopkins University Press, 1990).

14. *Encyclopedia of Greater Philadelphia,* s.v. "Greater Philadelphia Movement," by Carolyn T. Adams, 2016.

15. G. Terry Madonna and John Morrison McLarnon III, "Reform in Philadelphia: Joseph S. Clark, Richardson Dilworth, and the Women Who Made Reform Possible, 1947–1949," *Pennsylvania Magazine of History and Biography* 127 (January 2003): 57–88; Kirk R. Petshek,

The Challenge of Urban Reform: Politics and Programs in Philadelphia (Philadelphia: Temple University Press, 1973); Carolyn T. Adams, David Bartelt, David Elesh, Ira Goldstein, Nancy Kleniewski, and William Yancey, *Philadelphia: Neighborhoods, Division, and Conflict in a Post-industrial City* (Philadelphia: Temple University Press, 1991).

16. *The Better Philadelphia Exhibition: What City Planning Means to You* (Philadelphia: City Planning Commission, 1947); David W. Bartelt, "Renewing Center City Philadelphia: Whose City? Which Public Interest?" in *Unequal Partnerships: Political Economy of Urban Redevelopment in Postwar America,* ed. Gregory D. Squires (New Brunswick, NJ: Rutgers University Press, 1989), 80–102; Gregory L. Heller, *Ed Bacon: Planning, Politics, and the Building of Modern Philadelphia* (Philadelphia: University of Pennsylvania Press, 2013).

17. Charlene Mires, *Independence Hall in American Memory* (Philadelphia: University of Pennsylvania Press, 2002), chap. 8; Conn, *Metropolitan Philadelphia,* 83–86.

18. Guian A. McKee, "Blue Sky Boys, Professional Citizens, and Knights-in-Shining-Money: Philadelphia's Penn Center Project and the Constraints of Private Development," *Journal of Planning History* 6 (February 2007): 48–80; Heller, *Bacon,* chap. 4.

19. Heller, *Bacon,* chap. 5; Carolyn Adams, "Urban Governance and the Control of Infrastructure," *Public Works Management and Policy* 11, no. 3 (January 2007): 166–168; Philadelphia Redevelopment Authority, *Society Hill: A Modern Community That Lives with History* (Philadelphia, n.d.); Roman A. Cybriwsky, David Ley, and John Western, "The Political and Social Reconstruction of Revitalized Neighborhoods," in *Gentrification of the City,* ed. Neil Smith and Peter Williams (Boston: Allen and Unwin, 1986), 92–120; Stephanie R. Ryberg, "Historic Preservation's Urban Renewal Roots: Preservation and Planning in Midcentury Philadelphia," *Journal of Urban History* 39 (March 2013): 193–213; Neil Smith, *The New Urban Frontier: Gentrification and the Revanchist City* (London: Routledge, 1996), chap. 6. See also Bacon's obituary: "Edmund Bacon, 1910–2005," *Philadelphia Inquirer,* October 15, 2005.

20. Bauman, *Public Housing.* Some blocks leveled for urban renewal remain empty sixty years later.

21. Guian A. McKee, "Liberal Ends through Illiberal Means: Race, Urban Renewal, and Community in the Eastwick Section of Philadelphia, 1949–1990," *Journal of Urban History* 27 (July 2001): 574–583; U.S. Bureau of the Census, 2010–2014 American Community Survey 5-Year Estimates, Social Explorer, available at http://www.socialexplorer.com/; see also Eastwick Friends and Neighbors Coalition, https://eastwickfriends.wordpress.com/about/.

22. *Encyclopedia of Greater Philadelphia,* s.v. "Football: Professional," by John Maxymuk, 2015, and "Stadiums and Arenas," by Guian McKee, 2015.

23. Edwin Wolf II, "Epilogue," in Weigley, *Philadelphia,* 740–741; Carolyn T. Adams, "The Philadelphia Experience," *Annals of the American Academy of Political and Social Science* 551 (May 1997): 222–234.

24. Adams et al., *Philadelphia,* 37 and fig 2.1; Thomas R. Winpenny, "The Subtle Demise of Industry in a Quiet City: The Deindustrialization of Philadelphia, 1965–1995," *Essays in Economic and Business History* 16 (1998): 239–249.

25. McKee, *Problem of Jobs,* chaps. 1–3, 8.

26. U.S. Department of Transportation, Bureau of Transportation Statistics, Table 1-57: Tonnage of Top 50 U.S. Water Ports, http://www.rita.dot.gov/bts/sites/rita.dot.gov.bts/files/publications/national_transportation_statistics/html/table_01_57.html.

27. Adams et al., *Philadelphia,* 32–33; Winpenny, "Subtle Demise of Industry"; William J. Stull and Janice Fanning Madden, *Post-Industrial Philadelphia: Structural Changes in the Metropolitan Economy* (Philadelphia: University of Pennsylvania Press, 1990).

28. Philadelphia City Planning Commission, *Housing Characteristics: 1960 and 1970 Philadelphia Census Tracts* (Philadelphia, n.d.).

29. Hillier, "Who Received Loans"; *Encyclopedia of Greater Philadelphia*, s.v. "Redlining," by Kristen B. Crossney, 2016. Suburbanites who worked in Philadelphia paid the city payroll tax.

30. Philadelphia City Planning Commission, *Philadelphia's First Expressway* (Philadelphia, 1949); John F. Bauman, "The Expressway 'Motorists Loved to Hate': Philadelphia and the First Era of Postwar Highway Planning, 1943–1956, *Pennsylvania Magazine of History and Biography* 115 (October 1991): 503–533.

31. *Encyclopedia of Greater Philadelphia*, s.v., "Crosstown Expressway," by Sebastian Haumann, 2015, and "South Street," by Dylan Gottlieb, 2015.

32. Teaford, *Rough Road,* 165; Adams, "Urban Governance and the Control of Infrastructure," 173.

33. Cutler, "Persistent Dualism," 258–259; Joseph Gyourko and Anita A. Summers, "Philadelphia: Spatial Economic Disparities," in *Sunbelt/Frostbelt: Public Policies and Market Forces in Metropolitan Development,* ed. Janet Rothenberg Peck (Washington, DC: Brookings Institution Press, 2005), 110–139; Joel Garreau, *Edge City: Life on the New Frontier* (New York: Doubleday, 1991); U. S. Bureau of the Census, *1980 Census of Population and Housing: Census Tracts Philadelphia, PA.–N.J.,* report PHC80–2-283 (Washington, DC: Government Printing Office, 1983).

34. A 1973 study estimated the Puerto Rican population at that time at 85,000: Juan A. Albino, "Report on the Puerto Ricans in the City of Philadelphia," June 1973, Hispanic Federation for Social and Economic Development collection, Historical Society of Philadelphia; my thanks to Alyssa Ribeiro for bringing this to my attention.

35. U.S. Bureau of the Census, Census of 1950, Social Explorer; U.S. Bureau of the Census, *1980 Census*; Pew Charitable Trust, "Philadelphia's Changing Middle Class: After Decades of Decline, Prospects for Growth," February 2014, 1, 4–8, available at http://www.pewtrusts.org/.

36. Philadelphia City Planning Commission, *1960 and 1970 Philadelphia Census Tracts: Socio-Economic Characteristics* (Philadelphia, n.d.), *1990 Census: Selected Tables Population and Housing Data: 1990 and 1980* (Philadelphia, 1991); McKee, *Problem of Jobs*, 115; Charles Abrams, *Home Ownership for the Poor: A Program for Philadelphia* (New York: Praeger, 1970), 27; Bauman, *Public Housing*, 84–86.

37. Victor Vazquez-Hernandez, "Pan-Latino Enclaves in Philadelphia and the Formation of the Puerto Rican Community," in Takenaka and Osirim, *Global Philadelphia,* chap. 4.

38. Bauman, *Public Housing*, chap. 7; Abrams, *Home Ownership.*

39. John F. Bauman, "Row Housing as Public Housing: The Philadelphia Story, 1957–2013," *Pennsylvania Magazine of History and Biography* 138 (October 2014): 425–456; Bauman, *Public Housing*, pt. 2; *Encyclopedia of Greater Philadelphia*, s.v. "Public Housing," by Bauman, 2012; Wolfinger, *Philadelphia Divided*, chap. 7.

40. Lisa Levenstein, *A Movement without Marches: African American Women and the Politics of Poverty in Postwar Philadelphia* (Chapel Hill: University of North Carolina Press, 2009).

41. McKee, *Problem of Jobs,* chaps. 3, 4, 8; Bauman, *Public Housing,* chap. 9.

42. Bauman, *Public Housing,* chap. 5.

43. Jordan Stanger-Ross, *Staying Italian: Urban Change and Ethnic Life in Postwar Toronto and Philadelphia* (Chicago: University of Chicago Press, 2009); Peter Binzen, *Whitetown, U.S.A.* (New York: Vintage Books, 1970); Peter H. Rossi, *Why Families Move: A Study in the Social Psychology of Urban Residential Mobility* (Glencoe, IL: Free Press, 1955).

44. "Negro Is Burned in Effigy by Crowd in Philadelphia," October 6, 1966; Irving Spiegel, "Harassed Negro Vows Not To Move," October 8, 1966; "9 Arrested in Philadelphia at Scene of Racial Unrest," October 9, 1966, *New York Times*; Binzen, *Whitetown, U.S.A.*, 86. On how Fishtown has changed, see Sandy Smith, "Confession: I'm Black, and I Used to Be

Afraid to Walk around Fishtown," *Philadelphia Magazine*, October 4, 2014, available at http://www.phillymag.com.

45. Wolfinger, *Philadelphia Divided*, chaps. 4, 7, 8; Stanger-Ross, *Staying Italian*, 45–57; Abigail Perkiss, *Making Good Neighbors: Civil Rights, Liberalism, and Integration in Postwar Philadelphia* (Ithaca, NY: Cornell University Press, 2014).

46. Wolfinger, *Philadelphia Divided*, chap. 7; Nate Silver, "The Most Diverse Cities Are Often the Most Segregated," *FiveThirtyEightEconomics*, May 1, 2015, available at http://fivethirtyeight.com/. In 2010 the metropolitan area ranked as the sixth most segregated in the country: John R. Logan and Brian J. Stults, *The Persistence of Segregation in the Metropolis: New Findings from the 2010 Census* (US2010 Project, 2011).

47. U.S. Congress, Senate, *Elementary and Secondary Education Act of 1965*, hearings before the Sub-committee on Education of the Committee on Education, Labor, and Public Welfare, pt. 5, prepared statement of Celia Pinkus (Washington, DC: Government Printing Office, 1965), 2879–2886; Matthew F. Delmont, *The Nicest Kids in Town: American Bandstand, Rock 'n' Roll, and the Struggle for Civil Rights in 1950s Philadelphia* (Berkeley: University of California Press, 2012), chap. 2; Levenstein, *Movement without Marches*, chap. 4; *Encyclopedia of Greater Philadelphia*, s.v. "Northeast Philadelphia," by Matthew Smalarz, 2014.

48. Matthew J. Countryman, *Up South: Civil Rights and Black Power in Philadelphia* (Philadelphia: University of Pennsylvania Press, 2006), introduction, chaps. 1, 3; McKee, *Problem of Jobs*, chaps. 4, 7.

49. *Encyclopedia of Greater Philadelphia*, s.v. "Columbia Avenue Riot," by Alex Elkins, 2014.

50. Carmen Teresa Whalen, *From Puerto Rico to Philadelphia: Puerto Rican Workers and Postwar Economies* (Philadelphia: Temple University Press, 2001), chaps. 5–7; John Kromer, *Neighborhood Recovery: Reinvestment Policy for the New Hometown* (New Brunswick, NJ: Rutgers University Press, 2000) 48–51; on the AMP, see http://www.apmphila.org/welcome.html.

51. John Morrison McLarnon III, "Philadelphia: From One-Party Rule to One-Party Rule" (paper presented at the Pennsylvania Historical Association annual meeting, Lebanon, PA, October 8, 2015); in the author's possession.

52. Adams, "Greater Philadelphia Movement"; James Sanzare, *A History of the Philadelphia Federation of Teachers, 1941–73* (Philadelphia: Philadelphia Federation of Teachers, 1977), chap. 2. For a profile of Kensington schools in the late 1960s see Binzen, *Whitetown, U.S.A.*, 79, 155.

53. S. A. Paolantonio, *Frank Rizzo: The Last Big Man in Big City America* (Philadelphia: Camino Books, 1993).

54. Paolantonio, *Frank Rizzo*, pt. 2; Carol Jenkins, "The Miracle or Mirage of Local Governance? Mayor Rendell and the Philadelphia Fiscal Crisis" (Ph.D. diss., Temple University, 2001); Ryan, *AFSCME's Philadelphia Story*, 197.

55. *Rocky*, directed by John G. Avidson (United Artists, 1976); Conn, *Metropolitan Philadelphia*, 216. On the film's fortieth anniversary *Philadelphia Magazine* wrote: "for better or for worse, our city's identity is intractably entwined with Hollywood's most beloved underdog story," Victor Fiorillo, "Rocky: An Oral History," December 3, 2016, available at http://www.phillymag.com.

56. Teaford, *Rough Road to Renaissance*.

57. On wage tax's effect on jobs, see Philadelphia Jobs Growth Coalition, http://www.philadelphiagrowthcoalition.com/; Jared Brey, "Philly Workers and Businesses Might Get a Big Tax Cut . . . in Two Years," *Philadelphia Magazine*, July 20, 2016, available at http://www.phillymag.com/.

Chapter 5

1. U.S. Bureau of the Census, 2012 Economic Census, available at http://factfinder.census.gov/. In 2015, more than forty thousand residents worked in manufacturing, but half of those jobs were outside the city, U.S. Bureau of the Census, 2011–2015 American Community Survey 5-Year Estimates. The four Rust Belt cities listed each lost at least half their population from 1950–2000.

2. U.S. Bureau of the Census, 2012 Economic Census; U.S. Bureau of the Census, 2011–2015, American Community Survey 5-Year Estimates; Center City District and Central Philadelphia Development Corporation, *State of Center City Philadelphia 2016* (Philadelphia, 2016), available at http://www.centercityphila.org/socc/.

3. Center City District, *State of Center City;* Winpenny, "Subtle Demise of Industry"; U.S. Bureau of the Census, Decennial Census, 2000, Social Explorer.

4. Gerald Perrins and Diane Nilson, "Industry Shifts over the Decade Put Philadelphia on a New Road to Job Growth," *Monthly Labor Review,* April 2010, 3–18; Philadelphia City Planning Commission, *City Stats: General Demographic and Economic Data,* January 2005, www.phila.gov/cityplanning; Gyourko and Summers, "Philadelphia: Spatial Economic Disparities." For a more detailed discussion of this era, see Roger D. Simon and Brian Alnutt, "Philadelphia, 1982–2007: Toward the Postindustrial City," *Pennsylvania Magazine of History and Biography* 132 (October 2007): 395–444.

5. McLarnon, "Philadelphia," 11; Michael Schaffer, "The Worst Legislative Body in the World?" *Philadelphia Magazine,* April 30, 2010; Conn, *Metropolitan Philadelphia,* 20–21.

6. Jenkins, "Miracle or Mirage," chap. 3; John F. Bauman, "W. Wilson Goode: The Black Mayor as Urban Entrepreneur," *Journal of Negro History* 77 (Summer 1992): 141–158; Robert P. Inman, "How to Have a Fiscal Crisis: Lessons from Philadelphia," *American Economic Review* 85 (May 1995): 378–383.

7. Conn, *Metropolitan Philadelphia,* 217–220; John Hurdle, "A City Uses Murals to Bridge Differences," *New York Times,* October 7, 2008; see also Mural Arts Philadelphia, http://muralarts.org/.

8. Matthew Smalarz, "A Declaration of Independence: W. Wilson Goode, Hank Salvatore, and the Racial Politics of Urban Governance and Suburban Space" (paper presented at the Pennsylvania Historical Association annual meeting, Philadelphia, November 2014).

9. William K. Stevens, "Police Drop Bomb on Radicals' Home in Philadelphia," *New York Times,* May 14, 1985; John Anderson and Hilary Hevenor, *Burning Down the House: MOVE and the Tragedy of Philadelphia* (New York, 1987).

10. Jenkins, "Miracle or Mirage," chaps. 4–5; Ben Yagoda, "Mayor on a Roll: Ed Rendell," *New York Times,* May 22, 1994; Buzz Bissinger, *A Prayer for the City* (New York: Random House, 1997).

11. Bartelt, "Renewing Center City Philadelphia."

12. *Encyclopedia of Greater Philadelphia,* s.v. "SEPTA," by John Hepp, 2014; Center City District, *State of Center City.*

13. Adams, "Urban Governance," 173; Conn, *Metropolitan Philadelphia,* 15; Joel Mathis, "Convention Center Got Restraining Order against Carpenters Union," *Philadelphia Magazine,* February 9, 2015.

14. Eugenie Ladner Birch, "Having a Longer View of Downtown Living," *Journal of the American Planning Association* 68 (Winter 2002): 5–21; Philadelphia City Planning Commission, *Citywide Vision: Philadelphia 2035* (Philadelphia, 2013), 88; Center City District, *State of Center City.*

15. Peter Dorbin, "The Art of Politics," *Philadelphia Inquirer,* May 10, 2015; *Encyclopedia of Greater Philadelphia,* s.v. "Avenue of the Arts" and "Kimmel Center for the Performing Arts," by Dylan Gottlieb, 2015; see also Avenue of the Arts, http://www.avenueofthearts.org/; New Freedom Theater, http://www.freedomtheatre.org/; Center City Development Corporation, http://www.centercityphila.org/about/CPDC.

16. Previously, in succession, the Core States, First Union, and Wachovia Center.

17. Tommy Rowan, "What if the Phillies Ballpark Had Been Built in Central Philly?" *Philly.com,* April 28, 2016, http://www.philly.com; *Encyclopedia of Greater Philadelphia,* s.v. "Stadiums and Arenas," by Guian McKee, 2015; Barbara Ferman, "Leveraging Social Capital," in *Social Capital in the City: Community and Civic Life in Philadelphia,* ed. Richardson Dilworth (Philadelphia: Temple University Press, 2006), chap. 4.

18. Nathaniel R. Popkin, *Song of the City: An Intimate Portrait of the American Urban Landscape* (New York: Four Walls Eight Windows, 2002), 97–110; Stephen E. Nepa, "The New Urban Dining Room: Sidewalk Cafes in Postindustrial Philadelphia," *Buildings and Landscapes: Journal of the Vernacular Architecture Forum* 18 (Fall 2011): 60–81; Pew Charitable Trust, "Philadelphia's Changing Neighborhoods: Gentrification and other Shifts since 2000," May 2016, available at http://www.pewtrusts.org/en.

19. John L. Pickett and Mark Frazier Lloyd, "Penn's Great Expansion: Postwar Urban Renewal and the Alliance between Private Universities and the Public Sector," *Pennsylvania Magazine of History and Biography* 137 (October 2013): 381–430; Harley F. Etienne, *Pushing Back the Gates: Neighborhood Perspectives on University-Driven Revitalization in West Philadelphia* (Philadelphia: Temple University Press, 2012); Judith Rodin, *The University and Urban Renewal: Out of the Ivory Tower and Into the Streets* (Philadelphia: University of Pennsylvania Press, 2007).

20. Carolyn Adams David Bartelt, David Elesh, and Ira Goldstein, *Restructuring the Philadelphia Region: Metropolitan Divisions and Inequality* (Philadelphia: Temple University Press, 2008), 26; Center City District, *State of Center City*; Nepa, "New Urban Dining Room," 60–81; Conn, *Metropolitan Philadelphia,* 21; Pew Charitable Trust, "A Portrait of Philadelphia Migration: Who Is Coming to the City—and Who Is Leaving," July 2016, available at http://www.pewtrusts.org.

21. Paul R. Levy and Roman A. Cybrewsky, "The Hidden Dimensions of Culture and Class: Philadelphia," in *Back to the City: Issues in Neighborhood Renovation,* ed. Shirley B. Laska and Daphne Spain (New York: Pergamon Press, 1980), 138–155; Judith Goode and Robert T. O'Brien, "Whose Social Capital? How Economic Development Projects Disrupt Social Relations," and Patricia Stern Smallacombe, "Rootedness, Isolation, and Social Capital in an Inner City White Neighborhood," in Dilworth, *Social Capital in the City,* chaps. 8 and 9; Edward L. Crow, *Paths and Pitfalls: On the Way to a New Vibrancy in Older Retail Districts* (Pittsburgh: Dorrance, 2003); Lei Ding, Jackelyn Hwang, and Eileen Divringi, "Gentrification and Residential Mobility in Philadelphia," December 2015, and Seth Chizeck, "Gentrification and Changes in the Stock of Low-Cost Rental Housing in Philadelphia, 2000 to 2014," December 2016, Federal Reserve Bank of Philadelphia, available at www.philadelphiafed.org/.

22. Jenkins, "Miracle or Mirage," 166–172; City of Philadelphia, Office of the Controller, *An Analysis of the Keystone Opportunity Zone Program, 1999-2012: The Costs and Benefits to Philadelphia* (Philadelphia, 2014); Center City Development Corporation, *Center City Reports: Center City's Office Sector: Restarting the Engine of Growth* (Philadelphia: Center City Development Corporation, 2005); Adams et al., *Restructuring the Philadelphia Region,* chap. 2.

23. Dianna Marder, "Out of Fashion—Strawbridge and Closure," *Philadelphia Inquirer,* May 21, 2006; James Jennings, "The Secret Plans for the Gallery Have Finally Been Re-

vealed," *Philadelphia Magazine*, April 15, 2015. CCD defines "Greater Center City" as the area from Girard Avenue to Tasker Street between the rivers, far larger than the boundaries of the CCD itself.

24. Audrey Singer, Domenic Vitiello, David Park, and Michael Katz, "Recent Immigration to Philadelphia: Regional Change in a Re-Emerging Gateway," Brookings Institution, November 2008, available at http://www.brookings.edu/; Takenaka and Osirim, *Global Philadelphia*; Michael Matza, "Controversy follows Puerto Rican Migration," *Philly.com,* November 9, 2015; U.S. Bureau of the Census, American Community Survey, 2015 1-Year Estimate, Social Explorer. Non-Hispanics of other races or multiple races accounted for an additional 2.7 percent of the population.

25. City of Philadelphia, City Planning Commission, census track maps showing distribution of foreign born by country of birth, 2007–2011, December 2013 (AC120413); Jake Riley, "Immigrant Communities of Philadelphia: Spatial Patterns and Revitalization," Social Science Studio Reports, University of Pennsylvania, 2015, available at http://repository.upenn.edu/socialsciencestudio_reports/1; Singer et al., "Recent Immigration."

26. Lena Size, "Opportunity, Conflict, and Communities in Transition," in Takenaka and Osirim, *Global Philadelphia*, chap. 5; Wilson, *Ethnic Renewal,* chaps. 2–4.

27. Jennifer Lee, "Comparative Disadvantage of African American Owned Enterprise," in Dilworth, *Social Capital in the City*, chap. 7; David D. Kallick, "Bringing Vitality to Main Street: How Immigrant Small Businesses Help Local Economies Grow," Americas Society and Council of the Americas, January 2015, available at http://www.as-coa.org.

28. Takenaka and Osirim, *Global Philadelphia*, 198; Adams, "Philadelphia Experience"; Philadelphia Commission on Human Relations, *Widening the Circle of Our Concern: Public Perceptions of the School District of Philadelphia's Response to Intergroup Conflicts* (Philadelphia, n.d.).

29. Pew Charitable Trust, "The State of the City, A 2016 Update," March 2016, "Philadelphia's Changing Middle Class," and "Philadelphia's Changing Neighborhoods," available at http://www.pewtrusts.org/en.

30. Carolyn Teich Adams, "Homelessness in the Postindustrial City: Views from London and Philadelphia," *Urban Affairs Quarterly* 21 (1986): 527–549; Project HOME, https://projecthome.org/about/facts-homelessness.

31. Pew Charitable Trust, "Philadelphia's Changing Middle Class" and "Portrait of Philadelphia Migration"; Kristin A. Graham, "Ten Years Later: 'Dropout Crisis' Improves," May 20, 2015, Graham, "City to Harrisburg: Give More Money to Schools," July 3, 2015, and editorial, "Schools and the SRC," April 21, 2015, *Philadelphia Inquirer*; Susan De Jarnatt, "Community Losses: The Costs of Education Reform," 45 *University of Toledo Law Review* 579 (2014).

32. Bauman, "Row Housing as Public Housing," 453–456; Jon Hurdle, "To Rebuild a Neighborhood, Philadelphia Goes Beyond Housing, *New York Times,* May 3, 2016.

33. Pew Charitable Trust, "State of the City"; Matthew Friedman, Nicole Fortier, and James Cullen, "Crime in 2015: A Preliminary Analysis," November 2015, Brennan Center for Justice, available at www.brennancenter.org/.

34. Don Terry, "Philadelphia Shaken by Criminal Police Officers," *New York Times,* August 28, 1995; Sam Wood, "Exclusive: Shootings by Philly Police Soar as Violent Crime Plummets," *Philly.com*, May 14, 2013; George Fachner and Steven Carter, *An Assessment of Deadly Force in the Philadelphia Police Department*, Collaborative Reform Initiative (Washington, DC: Office of Community Oriented Policing Services, U.S. Department of Justice, 2015); Alice Goffman, *On the Run: Fugitive Life in an American City* (New York: Picador, 2014).

35. Mike Mallowe, "Notes from the New White Ghetto," *Philadelphia Magazine,* December 1986; Adams et al., *Restructuring the Philadelphia Region,* chap. 3; Kromer, *Neighborhood Recovery.*

36. Judith Goode and JoAnne Schneider, *Reshaping Ethnic and Racial Relations in Philadelphia: Immigrants in a Divided City* (Philadelphia: Temple University Press, 1994); Robert J. Stokes, "Business Improvement Districts and Inner City Revitalization: The Case of Philadelphia's Frankford Special Services District," *International Journal of Public Administration,* 29, nos. 1–3 (2006): 173–186.

37. Domenic Vitiello, "Twenty-First Century Urban Renewal in Philadelphia: The Neighborhood Transformation Initiative and its Critics," Planners Network, January 22, 2007, available at http://www.plannersnetwork.org; Stephen J. McGovern, "Philadelphia's Neighborhood Transformation Initiative: A Case Study of Mayoral Leadership, Bold Planning, and Conflict," *Housing Policy Debate* 17, 3 (January 2006): 529–570.

38. Ira Goldstein, "Subprime Lending, Mortgage Foreclosures and Race: How Far Have We Come and How Far Have We to Go?" The Reinvestment Fund, 2008, available at https://www.reinvestment.com/; Crossney, "Redlining."

39. U.S. Bureau of Labor Statistics, Economy at a Glance, Philadelphia City/County, available at https://www.bls.gov/eag; U.S. Bureau of the Census, American Community Survey, 2015, 1-Year Estimates; Richard Florida, "The Uneven Growth of High and Low-Wage Jobs Across America," *CityLab,* September 27, 2013, available at http://www.citylab.com/work/, and "The Boom Towns and Ghost Towns of the New Economy," *Atlantic,* October 2013, available at http://www.theatlantic.com.

40. Pew Charitable Trust, "The Fiscal Landscape of Large U.S. Cities," December 2016, available at http://www.pewtrusts.org/; Emma Brown, "In 23 States, Richer School Districts Get More Local Funding than Poorer Districts," *Washington Post,* March 12, 2015; Aubrey Whelan, "Alarms Sounded over Philadelphia Fire Department's Aging Fire Trucks and Ambulances," *Philadelphia Inquirer,* August 16, 2015; Patrick Kerkstra, "Michael Nutter Looks Back," *Philadelphia Magazine,* December 2015, available at http://www.phillymag.com.

41. "Poor People Can't Wait,*" Philadelphia Inquirer,* April 24, 2015; Jon Hurdle, "Philadelphia Raises Stakes with Plan to Reverse Blight," September 22, 2013, and Michael D. Shear, "U.S. Budgets Funds to Treat Heroin Abuse in Northeast," August 18, 2015, *New York Times*; Aubrey Whelan, "Homicides on the Rise in Philadelphia; Fewer Cases Solved," *Philadelphia Inquirer,* January 3, 2016.

42. Niccole Scott, "Philadelphia's New Boom," *Philadelphia Magazine,* March 1, 2015; Jacob Adelman, "The Resurgence of Center City Fueling Philly's Evolution," *Philadelphia Inquirer,* August 27, 2016.

INDEX

Page numbers in *italics* refer to illustrations.

Republican Party: defeat of, 81; dominance of, 46, 69; New Deal and, 76, 78; political machine and, 67–68
Reyburn, John, 56, 59–60
Richard Allen Homes, 76, *117. See also* Philadelphia Housing Authority (PHA); Public housing
Richmond, 28, 35, 38, 62
Ripka, Joseph, 25–26, *26*
Rittenhouse Square, 3, 32, 64, 66
Rizzo, Frank: early career, 98–99; as mayor, 99–100, 103; post-mayoral career, 104, 106
Rocky, 100, 138n55
Roosevelt, Franklin D., 76, 78
Roosevelt (formerly Northeast) Boulevard, 56, *57,* 69, 72
Ross, Betsy, 11
Rouse, Willard, III, 107
Roxborough, 25, 90

Schuylkill Banks Boardwalk, 121
Schuylkill Expressway, 91–92
Sesquicentennial International Exposition, 73, 88
Settlement patterns: from colonial era to 1800, 3, 4, *19,* 20; 1800–1865, 28, *29,* 30, 35, 38, *48*; 1865–1930, 52–57, 66; post–World War II, 90; racial segregation and, 96–97; in twenty-first century, 114
Shipbuilding industry, 5, 27, 50–51, 70, 71
Skyscrapers, 53–54, 107
Slaves and slavery, 4, 5, 11–13, 14–15, 17, 45. *See also* Abolition movement; African Americans
Slavic immigration, 61, 62–63
Society Hill, 82, *83,* 84, 86–87, 92
South Philadelphia, 73, 76; immigrants in, 61, 113; racial segregation in, 96–97. *See also other neighborhoods*
South Street, 82, 92
Southeastern Pennsylvania Transportation Authority (SEPTA), 92–93, 94, 107
Southwark, 14, 18, 28, 35, 43; African Americans in, 36, 92; gentrification of, 109; highways through, 92; houses in, *34;* immigrants in, 34, 38, 61; industry in, 27, 35, 50, 61; riots in, 38–39. *See also* Highways

Sports, professional and venues, 70, 88, 108–109, 114. *See also* Entertainment
Spring Garden district, 28, 30
State House, 16, 17, 20. *See also* Independence Hall
State Police, 59–60, *60*
Steffens, Lincoln, 67
Strawberry Mansion, 66, *98*
Street, John, 106, 119
Streetcars and trolleys. *See* Mass transit; Settlement patterns
Streets: conditions of, 8, 28; scenes of, *6, 7, 10, 31, 55*
Suburbs and suburbanization: population in, 93, 125; after World War II, 89, 91, 93–94, 96, 100, 103, 106, 115
Sullivan, Rev. Leon, 97

Tacony Creek park, 56
Tasker Homes, 76–77
Tate, James H. J., 99
Telegraph, 31
Textile industry, 25–26, 37, 38, 49–50, 59, 72, 79
Tourism, 82, 84, 108
Transportation. *See* Highways; Mass transit; Suburbs and suburbanization

University City, 109–110, 113
University of Pennsylvania (College of Philadelphia): founding of, 9; and medical education, 27; role in gentrification, 109–110; and urban renewal, 87
Urban renewal, 87, 90. *See also* Center City business district; University of Pennsylvania (College of Philadelphia)

Vare, William, 69
Vigilant Association, 37
Vine Street Expressway, *83,* 92, 113

War on Poverty, 95
Washington Square, 3
Welfare. *See* Public assistance and charity
Welfare capitalism, *49,* 60–61
West Philadelphia, 27, 28, 66, 72, 94, 96
Whig Party, 44, 45
White, Josiah, 24
Whitman Park, 100

ROGER D. SIMON is a Professor of History at Lehigh University. He is the author of *The City-Building Process: Housing and Services in New Milwaukee Neighborhoods, 1880–1910* and co-author of *Lives of Their Own: Blacks, Italians, and Poles in Pittsburgh, 1900–1960*.